NORTH WOODS
Cottage
COOKBOOK

JERRY MINNICH
ILLUSTRATIONS BY ERIKA REISE

TRAILS BOOKS
Black Earth, Wisconsin

Library of Congress Control Number: 2004116029
ISBN: 1-931599-55-6

Editor: Stan Stoga
Illustrations: Erika Reise
Design: Jennifer Jackson, Kathie Campbell

Printed in the United States of America by Sheridan Books

10 09 08 07 06 05   6 5 4 3 2 1

TRAILS BOOKS
A division of Trails Media Group, Inc.
P.O. Box 317 • Black Earth, WI 53515
(800) 236-8088 • e-mail: books@wistrails.com
www.trailsbooks.com

In memory of Virginia and Henry Morton, with thanks to Sue Lloyd,
who made the North Woods cottage experience possible for me.

Contents

Introduction

AH, SUMMERTIME AT THE COTTAGE—crystal sparkling water, the breeze whispering through pines, the plaintive call of the loon, the familiar drone of the mosquito. Then, autumn, glorious autumn, when the sugar maples turn ablaze, the sun casts a golden haze over forest and field, and the distant (or not-so-distant) sounds of gunfire echo softly across the lake. Winter is quiet time, time for roaring blazes in the cottage fireplace, time for hearty stews and mulled hot cider, time to check again and see whether the pipes have burst in the crawlspace under the back porch. Spring? Well, spring is generally a mess, but it is fun to gather fresh fiddleheads, watercress, and young dandelion leaves for a salad, to watch the ice recede from the lakeshore, to await the return of the loons, and to try to discover the source of that awful smell in the back bedroom.

Every season at the cottage is a special season, and all have one thing in common. That's right—food. Summer, fall, winter, or spring, we eat food pretty much every day. At home, we have our kitchen routines pretty well set—our favorite recipes, our well-appointed kitchen with the familiar pots and pans, the coffeemaker, the microwave, the convection oven, the food processor, blender, waffle iron, yogurt-maker, bread-maker, sandwich-toaster, tilt-head mixer, salad-spinner, pastry-blender, spice-grinder, milkshake machine, ice-crusher, fat separator, olive pit corer, juicer, bagel-toaster, electric tortilla press, snow cone maker, cherry-pitter, turkey-fryer, electric wok, crock pot, toaster oven, dog-groomer, chicken-plucker, and other kitchen aids and appliances without which any home cook would be totally helpless.

Up at the cottage, however, you will probably want to cut back somewhat on the number of appliances, perhaps of practical necessity. Many cooks could get along with a fraction of the equipment mentioned above. Many guys at deer camp, in fact, are able to get by just fine with a can opener and a butane lighter. The point is, you want to eat well at the cottage, but you may be forced to revert to earlier, more primitive, cooking methods. For instance, your great-grandmother was forced to live her entire life without a George Foreman Lean Mean Grilling Machine—yet she fed a family of eight with little thought or concern. You can do the same, if you just call upon the pioneer American spirit that lies deeply hidden within each of us.

To survive in the cottage kitchen, therefore, you need recipes that do not call for equipment you do not have. If the kids want Mickey Mouse waffles, you may have to give them pancakes and sharp knives and tell them to make their own. Further, you need recipes that do not require your presence in the kitchen for hours on end. It is much better to be swimming, or reading a trashy novel in the hammock, while the Meatball Surprise simmers gently on the stove. You need recipes that do not call for exotic ingredients that Harold and the Missus don't have down at the village grocery. ("Rossellino Pecorino? Sorry—how about Kraft Singles?") And you need recipes that are not too difficult to conceive or produce, since you will occasionally want to turn over kitchen duties to someone else, someone who might lack your superb talent, great taste, and unfailing culinary experience.

I have attempted to include such recipes in this modest book. All of these recipes are ones that I am capable of making, myself—which is quite a telling criterion since I am not what you would call a gourmet chef. If I had a job in a restaurant, it would be as a dishwasher or a singing waiter. (My "O Sole Mio" has drawn expressions of surprise and awe.) Most of these recipes do not call for exotic ingredients, and many are extremely quick to prepare and to cook. Most have come from my personal recipe file, which I have been building for more than 30 years and for which I at last have some practical use, while others have been contributed by considerate friends whose kitchen skills I admire.

In addition, however, there are some time-consuming recipes that I have included especially to fill some of those long, rainy days at the cottage. And of these, some are good to prepare with kids, who may be really tired of playing Yahtzee, kicking each other, groaning about the lack of TV, and asking when the rain is going to stop. What kid wouldn't like to make his own peanut butter fudge? What kid wouldn't like to make his own wiener winks and pretend he's back in school, eating hot lunch in the cafeteria?

Acknowledgments

SPECIAL THANKS TO ALL OF MY FRIENDS who submitted cottage-tested recipes for this book—I hope the T-shirts fit—Caroline Beckett, Caroline Erickson, Pat Kirsop, Pat Lisi, Tim Lloyd, Mary Lorenzen, John Minnich, Catherine Tripalin Murray, Priscilla Murphy, Jim Novak, Larry Sperling, Bill Stokes, Connie Thompson, Teresa Werhane, and Ellen Zybill. Thanks also to William Bolcom, who has earned the love of cottage cooks everywhere with his inspiring song, "Lime Jell-O Marshmallow Cottage Cheese Surprise."

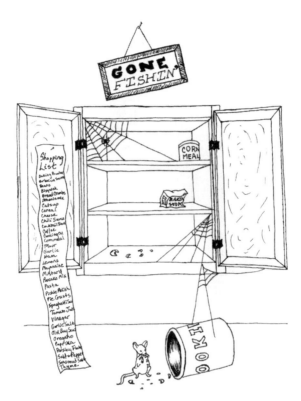

THE WELL-STOCKED
Cottage Cupboard

EVEN IF YOU PRIDE YOURSELF on being a
gourmet cook at home, there are certain shortcuts
you should be willing to adopt when vacationing at
the cottage. Face it, culinary standards are somewhat
more lax here in the North Woods, and priorities are
profitably rearranged. What would you rather be
doing at six o'clock in the evening — whipping up a
roux for the seafood-stuffed pasta shells, or watching
the loons on the lake with a gin and tonic in hand?

Ergo, you will swallow your pride and stock up on prepared spaghetti, chili, and barbecue sauces, premade piecrusts, soup mixes, bottled salad dressings, muffin mixes, and other convenience foods at which you would ordinarily turn up your patrician nose. But it's like killing chickens, folks. Once you slop some Cool Whip on the chocolate pudding pie with the prebaked crust for the first time, it gets easier after that.

Here are some essential items that any North Woods cottage should have, assuming you're going to be there for more than a week or so. Some you can bring from home because they might not be readily available at the local North Woods grocery. Others you can easily pick up after you've arrived and settled in — and you should do this, since the local economy depends upon your patronage during those few warm-weather months when tourists are sucking up the free sunshine and pine-scented air.

Stock Items

Baking powder
Barbecue sauce
Beans, canned (navy, kidney, garbanzo)
Bisquick
Bread crumbs
Brownie mix
Catsup
Cereal, breakfast
Cheese
Chili sauce
Cocktail sauce
Coffee
Cooking oil
Cornmeal
Flour, all-purpose
Garlic
Ham (large, bone-in)
Lemons, limes
Mayonnaise
Mustard
Pancake mix

Pasta
Pickle relish
Piecrusts, prepared
Rice
Salsa
Soups, canned and dry mixes (especially condensed cream of
  mushroom soup)
Spaghetti sauce
Tabasco sauce
Tea
Tomato juice or V8
Vinegar

Herbs and Spices

Many supermarkets now have little half-jars of common spices at
reasonable prices. They are perfect for stocking the cottage cupboard.
Garlic salt
Old Bay Seasoning
Oregano
Paprika
Parsley flakes
Salt and pepper
Seasoned salt
Thyme

Perishables to Buy at the
Local North Woods Grocery

Bread
Butter
Eggs
Hot dogs, brats, buns
Milk
Onions
Potatoes
Scallions
Sour cream
Whipped topping

MAKE IT UP Ahead

WHO WANTS TO SPEND A LOT OF TIME in the kitchen when you're up north? Here are a few recipes for dishes you can make at home, then take along to use as the occasion arises. It isn't hard to get up the enthusiasm to spend some hard kitchen time while you're at home anticipating the cottage experience—quite another to be stuck in the cottage kitchen while everybody else is swimming, hiking, playing golf, or snoring in a hammock.

Granola of the Gods

Make up a big batch of this superb granola and pack it in tight-sealing glass jars. Then all those early risers can make themselves a filling and nourishing breakfast while you sleep late. (Tell them not to slam the door on the way out.) This is also a good breakfast for the really late risers who stumble into the dining room just as the last of the bacon is disappearing.

Dry ingredients
10 cups rolled oats
1 cup brown sugar
1 cup whole wheat pastry flour
1½ cups grated coconut
1½ cups chopped pecans
1 cup dry milk

Wet ingredients
1 cup cooking oil
1 cup honey
2 eggs, beaten
1 tablespoon vanilla
1 teaspoon maple flavoring
½ cup water

Mix dry ingredients in a big bowl. Mix wet ingredients in a separate bowl. Combine. Stir well. Turn into two large, shallow baking pans. Heat in 200-degree oven for 30–40 minutes, stirring twice during baking. Remove from oven and stir once while cooling. Add raisins or dried cranberries if desired. Store in airtight container when cool. — *Teresa Werhane*

Six-Week Buttermilk-Bran Muffins

The following recipe was generously donated by Catherine Tripalin Murray, well-known Madison writer and author of *A Taste of Memories*. This recipe offers an easy way to feed a breakfast crowd with wholesome bran muffins—without getting up before sunrise! You can make up the batter at home, and it will keep for weeks in the cottage refrigerator. Just take the batter along to the cottage and bake off as needed. The recipe was originally passed along to Catherine by her tennis partner, Jan Homburg.

15-ounce box of Raisin Bran

2 cups granulated sugar
1 cup brown sugar
5 cups flour
5 teaspoons baking soda
2 teaspoons salt
4 teaspoons cinnamon
2 eggs, beaten
1 cup salad oil
1 quart buttermilk
Large can (29 ounce) fruit cocktail, drained

Mix cereal, sugar, flour, soda, salt, and cinnamon. Add beaten eggs, oil and buttermilk, and mix together well. Fold in drained fruit. Refrigerate overnight. Do not stir again. Fill greased muffin tins about ⅔ full. Bake at 400 degrees for 15–20 minutes. Dough will keep in refrigerator for six weeks. Makes 6–7 dozen muffins.

First-Night Beef Stew

For the first night at the cottage—before you've had a chance to get organized—count on this terrific beef stew. You can make it at home, several days ahead of time, then freeze it solid in a kettle. By the time you get to the cottage, it will be just partially thawed, and all you do then is heat and eat. You can double, or even triple, this recipe and have plenty of stew for the next few days' lunches.

2 tablespoons all-purpose flour
1 pound beef stew meat, or cubed round
2 tablespoons cooking oil
3½ cups V8 juice
½ cup chopped onion
1 small can beef broth
2 cloves minced garlic
½ teaspoon dried basil
½ teaspoon dried thyme
½ teaspoon dried oregano
½ teaspoon paprika
3 medium potatoes, cubed
3 medium carrots, sliced thick
1 cup celery, sliced

Coat beef cubes with flour in a sealed plastic bag. Brown beef in cooking oil in a large skillet. Remove beef to kettle. To kettle, add V8, beef broth, onion, garlic, and herbs. Bring to boil, then reduce heat and simmer 60–90 minutes. Add potatoes, carrots, and celery. Cover and simmer 30 minutes more. Let cool, then freeze. (Hint: If you have room in the kettle, you can cover the frozen stew with wax paper, then fill up the kettle with lemons, hot dogs, eggs, or anything you want to keep cool on your trip up north. Keep a tight lid on it.) Serves 4.

Minnich's Championship Chili

This is the chili recipe I have been using since 1960. It was the recipe of Senator John Tower (R-Tex.), who won the U.S. Senate chili contest with it, barely beating out Sen. Barry Goldwater (R-Ariz.). Over the years, I have adjusted the recipe to my personal taste and have never had any complaints (except that, sometimes, wimps think it's too spicy). Like my beef stew, you may easily double this recipe to serve more people. I make up the chili ahead and freeze it solid in a large stockpot. When we're packing to go to the cottage, I put wax paper over the frozen chili and fill up the rest of the pot with things I want to keep cool on the trip up north. I put the lid on tight, stow the pot in the car trunk, and by the time I get to the cottage the chili is just beginning to thaw.

Bacon fat
2 medium onions, chopped
4 cloves garlic, minced
1 or 2 green peppers
3 jalapeno peppers (fresh or canned)
2 pounds chuck or sirloin, cut in bite-size cubes
Small can tomato sauce
32-ounce can diced tomatoes
Chili powder to taste
Paprika to taste
1 tablespoon ground cumin
Dash oregano
Salt and pepper to taste
Splash of vinegar
Splash of Worcestershire sauce
32-ounce can kidney beans, drained

Grease a large iron pot or Dutch oven with bacon fat and sauté the onions, garlic, and peppers until soft but not browned. Add the meat and brown on all sides. Add the tomato sauce, four cans of water, and the tomatoes. Add the seasonings. Bring to a boil and simmer for about an hour. During the final cooking stage (or reheating at the cottage), add the beans and simmer for only 10 minutes more. Some purists don't add the beans at all, but I do. It makes the chili go further. Serves 6.

Don't Forget the Ham!

I always take a big bone-in ham along to the cottage. It makes a grand dinner, served with fresh potatoes and vegetables that you pick up at a roadside stand along the way, and then the leftover meat can be used in a number of ways for up to a week afterward—or as long as it lasts. In addition to ham sandwiches and ham-and-egg breakfasts, ham is a great base for soups, and I give several ham recipes later, in the "Soups" section.

Appetizers

FEW THINGS ARE MORE PLEASANT than cocktail hour on the pier, porch, or cottage lawn. Settle back in a chaise lounge, grasp a frosty gin and tonic—or lemonade, if you're so inclined—and watch the sun set as you discuss the Packers' chances against the Vikings, no-load double tax-free mutual funds, or ways to get rid of waxy yellow buildup on linoleum kitchen floors.

Of course, along with the libations you will want some appetizers—"nibbles," as our English cousins call them—to satisfy appetites while the ribs on the barbecue take ever so long to cook.

Here are some recipes for appetizers and nibbles that you can make in little time. Of course, you can go the easy route by ripping open a bag of potato chips and a dairy carton of French onion dip, but let's put a little effort into this, okay?

(Incidentally, here is a guy secret: You never need a bowl for potato chips. Simply lay the potato chip bag on its side, take a small knife, and cut a large section out of the bag, keeping about one-half inch from the edges. Voila! The bag becomes a bowl, you have one less dish to wash, and you become a host or hostess with not only perfect taste but also creativity and manual dexterity.)

Quick Vegetable Dip

The three-minute dip you can throw together when you see the boat coming back to the pier.

> 1 cup sour cream
> 1 cup mayonnaise
> 1 package dry onion soup mix
> Scallions

Blend all ingredients except scallions. Chill 1 hour or more. Garnish with chopped scallions and serve with fresh raw vegetables or potato chips.

Southwestern Vegetable Dip

For extra zip, add Tabasco sauce or buy hot salsa.

> 2 cups sour cream
> 1 package dry onion soup mix
> 1 cup medium-hot salsa
> Scallions

Blend all ingredients except scallions. Chill 1 hour or more. Garnish with chopped scallions and serve with fresh raw vegetables or corn chips.

Black Bean Dip

From Campbell's Kitchen, so it's got to be good.

1 can Campbell's black bean soup
½ cup chunky salsa
Shredded cheddar cheese
Sliced pitted black olives
Sliced scallions
Sour cream

Mix soup and salsa. Refrigerate at least 2 hours. Top with cheese, olives, onions, and sour cream. Serve with tortilla chips or fresh vegetables for dipping.

Chilled Green Beans

If you bring home a bunch of fresh green beans from the roadside stand, try this great recipe. It can serve as an appetizer or as a side dish with chicken or beef.

2 pounds fresh green beans
⅓ cup wine vinegar
1¾ cups olive oil
8 ounces roasted red pepper or pimiento
2 garlic cloves, minced
2 teaspoons basil
1 teaspoon oregano
1 teaspoon sugar
Salt to taste

Clean, remove ends, and boil the beans until crisp-tender, about 15 minutes. Transfer to ice water immediately to cool, then drain and place in a large bowl with all the other ingredients. Mix all very well, cover, and chill in refrigerator overnight.

Gringo's Seviche

Seviche (pronounced say-BEECH-ay) is popular bar food throughout Central America. I chowed down on it at a dusty roadside tavern in Costa Rica until someone told me it probably wasn't a good idea to eat raw fish in Central America. Still, it was great—and I survived. Served chilled, seviche is a great summertime appetizer, cool and refreshing.

    1 pound fresh whitefish, lake trout, or other fresh, firm, white fish
    ³/₄ cup fresh lemon juice
    1 large tomato, peeled and chopped
    ½ cup chopped onion
    ¼ cup chopped green pepper
    ¼ cup chopped fresh cilantro
    ¼ cup fresh lemon juice
    1 clove garlic, minced
    1 teaspoon salt
    ½ teaspoon Tabasco sauce
    1 tablespoon olive oil

Slice the fish into bite-size strips. Place them in a glass or ceramic bowl, add ³/₄ cup lemon juice, and mix well. Cover and refrigerate 6–8 hours. Then drain off liquid. Mix remaining ingredients and stir in with fish. Add in the remaining ¼ cup of lemon juice. Mix everything well and chill another couple of hours. Serves 6 as an appetizer.

Crunchy Chicken Legs

This is a good and easy recipe for serving at a party, or to feed a bunch of kids at lunch or dinner.

    ³/₄ cup butter, melted
    ³/₄ cup bread crumbs
    1 teaspoon Old Bay Seasoning (optional)
    3 tablespoons dry onion soup mix
    12 chicken legs

Preheat oven to 350 degrees. Mix together the bread crumbs and onion soup mix. Dip each chicken leg into melted butter, then roll in dry mixture. Place leftover butter into a baking pan and lay in the chicken legs. Bake 50–55 minutes, until chicken legs are done.

Baked Stuffed Mushrooms

You can make these in 15 minutes and they'll be ready in 30.

18 medium button mushrooms
3 ounces softened cream cheese
1/4 cup Parmesan cheese, grated
2 tablespoons milk
18 almond slices
1/4 cup melted butter

Preheat oven to 350 degrees. Wash mushrooms and remove stems. Cream together the cream cheese, Parmesan cheese, and milk. Fill the mushroom caps with the cheese mixture and top with an almond slice. Dip each mushroom in melted butter and place on a buttered baking pan. Bake 15 minutes or until tops are golden brown.

Party Time Meatballs

Is this an easy recipe or what? Serve to your guests with toothpicks and they'll swear they're at the office Christmas party. You could also get away with this recipe for dinner served over noodles, if you just call them Swedish meatballs. But expect a formal protest from the embassy.

2-pound package frozen precooked meatballs
1 cup chili sauce
1 cup honey barbecue sauce
1 cup grape jelly

Thaw and heat meatballs according to package directions. In saucepan combine the sauces and grape jelly and heat until well blended. Introduce the meatball to the sauce and—voila!—you have a really tacky appetizer.

Pina Colada Dip

This is a great, easy-to-make dip for any kind of fruit.

8-ounce can of crushed pineapple, with juice
3/4 cup milk
3-ounce package of instant coconut pudding/pie filling mix
1/2 cup sour cream

In a blender, blend all ingredients on medium for approximately 40 seconds. Chill for several hours or overnight and serve with fresh strawberries, melon, or other fruits.

Cheese Puffs

Once guests begin popping these into their mouths, they become hopelessly addicted. The platter will be cleaned out in minutes. And cheese puffs are not hard to make, either.

2 cups butter
1 pound sharp cheddar, cubed
4 cups sifted flour
1/2 teaspoon salt
1 teaspoon cayenne pepper
1/2 teaspoon paprika

Cut the butter and cheese into the flour with a pastry cutter or large fork. Add in the salt and cayenne. Roll out dough to about 1/4-inch, then cut into rounds with a shot glass. Sprinkle with paprika. Place on an ungreased cookie sheet and bake at 325 degrees for 12–15 minutes. Cool and serve.

BREAKFAST & BRUNCH
For a BUNCH

SURE, YOU CAN BE A SHORT-ORDER COOK and stand over a hot stove all morning, making up individual dishes. But here are some better ideas— breakfast recipes that you can cook up all at once, or that you can make up the night before and just pop in the oven in the morning.

Baked Eggs Chiffon

Here's one you can make up the night before. While it is baking in the morning, you can prepare bacon the easy way. Just put the bacon in a shallow baking dish lined with aluminum foil, and bake it in the oven along with the eggs.

     10 large eggs
     10 slices of bread
     1/2 cup butter, melted
     1 sweet red pepper, diced
     1 pound mushrooms, sliced
     Small bunch parsley, finely chopped
     2 cups milk
     1 1/2 cups grated Swiss cheese
     Salt and pepper to taste

Separate the eggs into two bowls. Remove crusts from the bread and cut the slices into 1/2-inch cubes. Sauté the pepper and mushrooms and set aside. Arrange the bread cubes in a 9x13-inch baking pan, pour the melted butter over the bread, and then distribute the pepper, mushrooms, cheese, and parsley over the bread cubes. Beat the egg yolks with milk, salt, and pepper and pour over the bread cubes. Beat the egg whites until they're stiff, then spread them over all the other ingredients, like you were icing a cake. Cover with foil and chill overnight. In the morning, uncover and bake at 315 degrees for 40–45 minutes, until eggs are firm. Serves 8–10.

Egg Scramble

The best way to serve a bunch of eggs to a bunch of people is to make an egg scramble. The choice of ingredients is limitless, and can include almost anything you have on hand—leftover ham or turkey, sausage, mushrooms, tomato, cheese, broccoli, zucchini, peppers, spinach, asparagus, onions, corned beef—you name it. Count on three eggs per person. The general rule is to beat the eggs with milk, using 1/2 cup of milk to every three eggs. Then, all the added ingredients should be bite-size in a ready-to-eat state, because the eggs will cook for only a few minutes. That means you may want to sauté things like mushrooms, onions, and most green vegetables before starting the eggs, while things such as leftover meats, green peppers, tomatoes, and cheese can go in as is.

Served with oven-baked potatoes, an egg scramble is a hearty breakfast, fortifying the best of us for a day of lying on the boat pier.

Easy Potatoes O'Brien

These are a perfect accompaniment to any egg dish. And nobody has to know you made them with frozen french fries.

⅓ cup chopped green pepper
2 tablespoons chopped pimento
1 medium onion, chopped
¼ cup butter
1 package (16 ounce) frozen French fried potatoes, diced
1 teaspoon salt
Pepper to taste

In a large skillet, sauté the green pepper, pimento, and onion in butter until onion is tender. Stir in potatoes, salt, and pepper. Cook until potatoes are brown, then serve. Serves 4.

Diner-Style Roasted Potatoes

The big problem many people have with roasted potatoes is that the bottoms blacken before the insides get done. This recipe answers that problem.

2 pounds white potatoes, unpeeled
3 tablespoons olive oil
2 teaspoons minced garlic
2 teaspoons dried oregano or rosemary
1 teaspoon seasoned salt
Black pepper to taste

Clean potatoes and cut them into bite-size chunks. Microwave them, full power, for 3 minutes, or, lacking a microwave at the cottage, boil them for 8 minutes to soften them up. Meanwhile, preheat the oven to 400 degrees. Toss the potato chunks with the oil, garlic, and seasonings. Line a baking pan with aluminum foil and spread out the potato chunks in the pan. Roast them for 35 minutes or until the outsides are golden brown and the innards are soft and steamy. Clean-up is a breeze. Serves 4–6.

Magic Popovers

Popovers are not difficult, says Larry Sperling. But they do require faith and confidence. Do you have the right stuff?

1⅔ cups skim milk
5 eggs
1⅔ cups all-purpose flour
2 tablespoons sweet butter, melted (plus more for greasing tins)
½ teaspoon salt

Butter 12 nonstick muffin cups. Set aside. Set oven rack to the center shelf and preheat oven to 400 degrees. Pour milk and eggs into a blender and blend for 5 seconds. Add melted butter, flour, and salt, and pulse another 5-8 seconds until frothy and smooth. Pour the batter into the cups, filling each about ⅔ to ¾ full. (You can make the batter up to a few hours ahead of time and just pulse it quickly before you pour it.)

Place the filled muffin tins in the center of the oven, close the oven door, and immediately reduce the temperature to 375 degrees. Bake 50 minutes and—here comes the faith part—do not open the oven door to peek during this time. Popovers rise by building steam within the batter, and you can make them fall by opening the door as they are baking. After 50 minutes the popovers should have risen well above the tin tops and be golden brown.

Remove the tins and let them cool. You can gently remove the popovers after a minute. Serve hot, within 15 minutes if possible. Lightly buttered or dabbed with jam, these are a real treat. Cooled popovers may be filled with tuna or chicken salad, but they are best served hot right out of the oven. Makes 12 popovers. —*Larry Sperling*

Italian Sausage Breakfast

This is an easy recipe, but it takes about 25 minutes of prep time and 50 minutes to bake. If there's an early riser in your group, give him the recipe the night before. In the morning, your nose will tell you when it's time to get out of bed.

6 medium potatoes, peeled and sliced ⅛-inch thick
2 medium onions, diced
2 sweet green peppers, diced

Salt
12 Italian sausage links

Preheat oven to 350 degrees. Lay the sliced potatoes in the bottom of a 9x13-inch baking pan. Cover with the diced onions and green pepper, and salt to taste. Pierce sausage links once each with a fork and lay them on top of the vegetables. Bake at 350 degrees for 30 minutes. Turn sausages over and bake for another 20 minutes. Serves 8–10.

Morel Mushrooms

I have seen all kinds of recipes for morels—stuffed morels, morels with linguini, morels in sour cream, etc.—but in truth, morels are so fantastic that I would not prepare them any other way but sautéed in butter, with perhaps a few drops of fresh lemon drizzled over them. If you are lucky enough to capture the wily morel, my congratulations and compliments to you.

Simply cut each morel in two, lengthways, run them quickly under cold water, pat dry with paper toweling, and sauté them quickly in melted butter. Serve them immediately. Indescribable with scrambled eggs in the morning.

Main Dishes

THE VERY BEST MAIN DISH is your favorite selection from the menu of the best restaurant in the area. The second-best is the entrée prepared at the cottage by someone else, preferably a friend who is also head chef at The Four Seasons. Third-best is a simple, hearty, and great-tasting dish prepared by you. Before settling for third best, however, be sure to strike your bargain: You will cook, someone else will clean up and wash the dishes, and still another will take care of breakfast in the morning. Sharpen your negotiating skills! That said, here are some good recipes that won't keep you in the kitchen all too long—and may even let you enjoy a cocktail with the other folks.

Easy Meat Loaf

Here's a quick and easy one. And if anybody says, "What, you're going to feed us meat loaf?" just reply that meatloaf is America's favorite comfort food.

  1 can condensed tomato soup
  2 pounds ground beef
  1 envelope dry onion soup mix
  ½ cup dry breadcrumbs
  1 egg, beaten
  ¼ cup water

Mix thoroughly ½ cup of the tomato soup, ground beef, onion soup mix, breadcrumbs, and egg. Shape firmly into a 9x5-inch loaf pan. Bake at 350 degrees for 1¼ hours or until done. Mix together 2 teaspoons of the drippings, the remaining tomato soup, and water in saucepan. Heat thoroughly and serve over the meat loaf. Serves 8.

Italian Meat Loaf

Here's another easy meatloaf, this one with an Italian accent.

  1½ pounds ground beef
  ¼ cup minced onion
  ½ teaspoon oregano
  ½ cup Italian bread crumbs
  1 egg, beaten
  ¼ cup water

Mix all ingredients thoroughly. Shape into loaf in bread pan. Bake for 1 hour at 350 degrees or until done. Roast whole potatoes along with meat loaf. Serves 6.

Snappy Meat Loaf

This recipe calls for just a few more ingredients, but turns out a truly delicious meat loaf.

  2 pounds ground beef
  1 cup finely chopped onion

24 Saltine crackers, crumbled
1 teaspoon salt
½ teaspoon black pepper
2 eggs, beaten
16 ounces tomato sauce
4 tablespoons cider vinegar
½ teaspoon dry mustard
4 tablespoons brown sugar

Knead together the ground beef, onion, crackers, salt and pepper, eggs, and 8 ounces of the tomato sauce. Shape firmly into a 9x5-inch loaf pan. Mix together the vinegar, dry mustard, and brown sugar and pour over the meat loaf. Bake at 350 degrees for 1¼ hours, until done. Serves 8.

Flank Steak with Mama Cole's Steak Sauce

You'll need some flank steak, butter, catsup, Worcestershire sauce, and chopped parsley for this one. The amounts are entirely up to you. (We can't do everything for you.)

Flank steak
Butter
Catsup
Worcestershire sauce
Fresh parsley

Grill a flank steak so it is rare inside—red, not pink. Slice it thinly (¼-inch) on the diagonal across the grain. Into a large skillet or other pan, dump a big lump of butter, some catsup, a few shakes of Worcestershire sauce, and a little chopped fresh parsley. Heat while stirring until butter melts and it begins to bubble. Add flank steak slices and sauté until steak is done to preference. Drizzle sauce over the steak just before serving. Mmmm. —*Priscilla Murphy*

Easiest-Ever Beef Roast

If it gets any easier than this, call me.

2–3 pound eye of round beef roast
Salt and pepper to taste

Preheat the oven to 500 degrees. Salt and pepper roast and put it on a rack in a shallow baking pan lined with foil. No cover, no water. Put roast in oven and reduce heat to 475 degrees. Roast at 7 minutes per pound. DO NOT OPEN OVEN DOOR. Then turn off oven and let roast sit inside oven for 2½ hours. REPEAT — DO NOT OPEN THE OVEN DOOR DURING THIS TIME. Go out on the pier, have a cocktail, and stop worrying. Serves 4–6.

How to Make Today's Beef Barbecue from Yesterday's Leftover Roast Beef

No problem. Serve this barbecue on buns for lunch, or for an evening cookout.

2 pounds cooked beef, shredded
1 large onion, finely chopped
1 medium green pepper, finely chopped
½ cup sweet pickle relish
1 teaspoon prepared mustard
½ teaspoon salt
2 cups of your favorite barbecue sauce
8 hamburger buns

Preheat oven to 350 degrees. Mix all the ingredients and bake in oven at 350 degrees for about 45 minutes. (I find that you can shred cooked beef with a hand potato masher.) Makes 8 sandwiches.

Sloppy Joes

You can double or triple this recipe for a big crowd. Kids love Sloppy Joes, but they aren't called sloppy for nothing. It's best to make the kids eat these sandwiches out on the lawn, and then to hose them off afterward. Works with Uncle Freddie, too.

1 pound ground beef
1 small chopped onion
1 small chopped green pepper
½ teaspoon garlic salt
12-ounce bottle chili sauce
Dash of Tabasco sauce
4 hamburger buns

Brown ground beef. Drain fat. Sauté onion and pepper until soft but not burned. Add other ingredients and simmer for 20 minutes. Serves 4.

Beef Barbecue

This is an easy recipe for a really good beef barbecue. Will serve a lot of people with little fuss.

4 pounds stew meat
1 medium onion, chopped
2 cups catsup
6 teaspoons prepared mustard
Vinegar
1 cup packed brown sugar
1 bottle oily French dressing
Salt and pepper
15 hamburger buns

Boil meat with onion for 3 hours. Drain off water and save some. When cool enough, break apart meat and pull off excess fat. Mix catsup, mustard, and vinegar to taste and bring to boil. Stir into meat. Add salad dressing and salt and pepper to taste and mix well. Serve warm on buns. Serves 10–15.

Hungarian Goulash

This recipe calls for a lot of ingredients, but it's not really hard to make, and the best thing about it is that the last two hours are totally task-free, letting you join the group for cocktails on the pier. Two hours? Maybe too many cocktails. Be careful.

> 2 pounds stewing beef
> 4 tablespoons cooking oil
> 3 medium onions, chopped
> 1 medium green pepper, sliced
> 1 medium tomato, peeled and sliced
> ½ teaspoon garlic powder
> 3 teaspoons paprika
> 1½ teaspoons salt
> 1½ teaspoons pepper
> 2 tablespoons tomato paste
> 1 can (14-ounce) beef broth
> 1 crumbled bay leaf
> ½ cup sour cream

In a heavy, deep skillet or Dutch oven, brown the beef in oil. Remove meat and, in the same oil, sauté the onion, pepper, tomato, and garlic powder, for about 3 minutes. Add in the other ingredients and bring to a boil. Cover, turn down heat, and simmer for about 2 hours, until meat is tender. Just before serving, stir in sour cream. Serve over broad buttered noodles. Serves 4–6.

Beef Stroganoff

Here's another good stew that calls for most of the work to be done well before dinnertime.

> 2 pounds beef fillet, sliced thin
> All-purpose flour
> 1 teaspoon salt
> ½ teaspoon black pepper
> 1 teaspoon paprika
> 1½ cups onion, chopped fine
> Cooking oil
> 2 cups sliced mushrooms
> 2 cups beef broth

1 tablespoon chopped chives
1 pint sour cream
1 pound egg noodles, cooked

Preheat oven to 350. Dredge sliced beef in flour seasoned with salt, pepper, and paprika. Sauté with onions in cooking oil in a deep baking pan until lightly browned. Add mushrooms and beef broth and cook until smooth. Add chives, transfer to a 350-degree oven, and bake until beef is tender, about 90 minutes. (Tougher cuts of beef will take longer.) Add sour cream, stir, and bake another 10 minutes. Serve over cooked noodles. Serves 4–6.

Pot Roast with Root Vegetables

This is a dependable, basic pot roast recipe. I like it with a good, heady horseradish. You can vary the vegetables, according to which and how many you have on hand.

3 ½ pounds beef chuck roast
Salt and pepper to taste
2 tablespoons bacon fat or vegetable oil
8 small onions, whole and peeled
2 medium carrots, peeled and cut into 1-inch lengths
3 medium parsnips, scrubbed and cut into 1-inch lengths
6 small turnips, scrubbed and halved
3 medium potatoes, scrubbed and quartered
1 teaspoon dried thyme
½ cup beef or chicken stock
½ cup dry red wine

Heat the oven to 325. Sprinkle the roast with salt and pepper and rub on all sides. Heat the fat in a Dutch oven over medium heat and brown the roast on all sides—10 minutes total. Remove the roast to a plate. Add all the vegetables and thyme, cover, and cook on medium-low for 10 minutes. Return the roast to the pan, add the stock, and bring to a boil. Cover the pot and move it to the oven. Cook until fork-tender, 2 ½ to 3 hours. Skim some fat from the sauce and, if necessary, boil the sauce to reduce it. To serve, slice the meat across the grain and serve with the juice and vegetables. Serve with good, heavy bread and either red wine or beer. Serves 6. —*John Minnich*

Flyfisher's Secret Pot Roast

Here's another great pot roast recipe, this one contributed by Steve Born, planner, environmental guru, and flyfisher extraordinaire. Steve attributes this successful recipe to his early years as bachelor, father of a hungry son, and sometimes cook at trout fishing camps.

3–5-pound chuck roast
1 can tomato soup
1 can (empty soup can) of red wine or beer
4–5 onions, peeled and halved
Potatoes, halved or small reds placed around roast
Can of water
Basil, salt, and pepper to taste
4 medium carrots

Put all ingredients, except carrots, in roasting pan. Halve carrots and lay lengthwise across top, making sure to spread some of the liquid mixture over them. Cover with aluminum foil (seal edges) and cook for about 2 hours in 350–375-degree oven. —*Steve Born*

Scalloped Potatoes with Leftover Meat

Wonder what to do with that leftover pot roast—or chicken, or pork, or venison, or turkey? Wonder no more. The Milwaukee County Extension Service comes to the rescue—providing that you can find some potatoes under the sink.

4 or 5 medium potatoes
1 medium onion
2 tablespoons all-purpose flour
1 teaspoon salt
¼ teaspoon pepper
1 tablespoon margarine or butter
1 cup cubed, cooked meat
1½ cups milk

Preheat oven to 350 degrees. Slice potatoes and onion into an 8x8-inch pan. Sprinkle with flour, salt, and pepper. Dot with margarine or butter. Add meat, stir lightly. Pour milk over all. Bake at 350 degrees for 20 minutes. Remove from oven and stir. Return to oven and bake 40 minutes longer, or until fork slides easily into potatoes. Good served with applesauce. Serves 4.

Swiss Steak

Don't blame me. Blame the Swiss.

  2 pounds round steak, cut ¾-inch thick
  1 tablespoon cooking oil
  2 cans condensed cream of mushroom soup
  1 large onion, chopped
  3 tablespoons steak sauce
  1 tablespoon soy sauce
  2 cloves garlic, minced
  8 medium potatoes

Preheat oven to 350. Pound the steak until you have conquered it and then cut it into serving-size pieces. Brown the pieces in the oil, in a skillet, then drain. Transfer the steak to a large baking pan. Combine the soup, onion, sauces, and garlic and pour over and around the meat. Put in the oven for 15 minutes at 350, while you peel the potatoes and cut them in half. Add the potatoes around edges of the pan, on top of the meat, and bake for another hour. Presto—you've got a meal in a pan. But serve on plates. Serves 4.

Chopstick Tuna Casserole

More fun with mushroom soup! Here's a quintessential comfort food recipe that you can double for a bigger crowd.

  1 can condensed cream of mushroom soup
  ¼ cup water
  2 cups chow mein noodles, broken up a little
  ¼ cup chopped onion
  ½ teaspoon salt
  ¼ teaspoon pepper
  1 can (6½–7 ounce) tuna, drained and flaked
  1 cup sliced celery

Preheat oven to 375 degrees. In a bowl, mix together the soup and water; then add the onion, pepper, tuna, and celery, and 1 cup of the chow mein noodles. Toss. Turn this mess into a shallow baking dish or pan. Scatter the remaining noodles over top and bake at 375 degrees for 30 minutes until bubbling and comforting. Serve with salad. Serves 4.

Easy Tuna Pasta

Nothin's easier than this one. Just be sure to use tuna packed in oil, not water.

    1 pound tortellini pasta
    2 cups frozen baby peas
    12-ounce can of tuna in oil
    Salt and pepper

Cook the tortellini in water until just about tender. Add peas and cook one more minute. Drain, return to pot, and add the tuna in its oil. (If you have some pimiento-stuffed green olives, you can slice a few and add them in, too.) Add salt and pepper to taste. Heat through, stirring gently, and serve. Serves 4.

Tex-Mex Meatball Soup

Here's a super-easy recipe from down El Paso way. Cowboys used to run to the chuck wagon when the triangle clanged on Thursday nights, because they knew that Thursday was "Tex-Mex Meatball Soup Night." Bet you never knew that.

    2 cans (14 ounces each) beef broth
    2 cups frozen corn
    1 cup salsa
    1 package fully cooked meatballs
    Cilantro (optional)
    Tortilla chips

Combine the broth, corn, and salsa in a saucepan. Bring to a boil and simmer for 5 minutes. Microwave the meatballs according to package directions. Add meatballs to soup mixture, top with chopped cilantro (optional), and serve with tortilla chips. Serves 4.

Cucumber Yogurt Soup

Here is a great noontime soup for a warm day up north. Mighty cooling, and easy to make, too.

2 cups unflavored yogurt
$1/16$ teaspoon dried mint, or one teaspoon finely chopped fresh mint
1 medium cucumber, peeled, deseeded, and chopped fine
1 cup cold water
Salt and pepper to taste

Blend all ingredients and chill in refrigerator for one hour or more. Garnish with fresh mint leaves, watercress, or chopped pecans. Serves 4.

Chicken Noodle Soup

Here's an easy recipe to use up that leftover chicken. If you have the remains of a whole chicken, boil it in enough water to cover the chicken, and add some chopped onions, celery, and carrots for flavor. Boil slowly for 40–60 minutes, then drain and discard the vegetables. Or, just use canned chicken broth or chicken base, prepared according to package directions.

2 quarts chicken stock or broth
1 tablespoon chopped fresh parsley, or $1/2$ teaspoon dried flakes
1 cup diced leftover cooked chicken
8-ounce package egg noodles
Salt and pepper to taste

Bring chicken stock or broth to a boil, then add the other ingredients. Bring back to a boil, then reduce heat to a slow boil and cook for about 15 minutes. Serve with good bread or crackers. Serves 6–8.

Chicken Vegetable Soup

Oh boy, another way to use up that leftover chicken. And you can use some of the fresh vegetables you picked up at the roadside stand, too. (Feel free to leave out some of the vegetables if you don't happen to have them on hand.)

        1 quart chicken broth or stock (see recipe above)
        1 cup diced leftover cooked chicken
        1 cup green beans
        2 medium potatoes, peeled and diced
        1 stalk celery, sliced
        ½ cup sliced mushrooms, fresh or canned
        1 medium onion, coarsely chopped
        2 carrots, peeled and sliced
        ½ cup fresh or canned corn
        Salt and pepper to taste

Add all the ingredients to the broth in a large saucepan or soup kettle. Bring to a boil, then reduce heat and simmer for 40 minutes. Adjust seasonings. Serves 4–6.

Johnny Marzetti

There are a million Johnny Marzetti recipes. This one is my favorite — better than most, easier than some.

        8-ounce package egg noodles
        2 tablespoons butter
        1 small onion, chopped
        1 clove garlic, minced
        1 pound lean hamburger
        6-ounce can tomato paste
        1 can water
        8-ounce can sliced mushrooms, undrained
        2 stalks celery, chopped
        1 green pepper, chopped
        1 teaspoon vinegar
        ½ pound grated cheddar or American cheese
        Salt and pepper to taste

Cook noodles until almost done. Melt butter in large, deep skillet and sauté onion and garlic until soft. Add hamburger, break apart, and cook until browned. Stir in tomato paste, water, mushrooms with liquid, celery, green pepper, vinegar, cheese, salt and pepper. Cook, covered, 30–45 minutes. Mix with noodles, top with a little extra grated cheese. Simmer for an additional 30 minutes, or bake in oven at 350 degrees for 30 minutes. Serves 4.

Three-Bean Casserole

A traditional Midwestern hot dish to pass. Perfectly suitable for any church social.

1 pound ground beef
½ pound uncooked bacon, diced
1 large onion, chopped
½ cup packed brown sugar
½ cup picante sauce or chili sauce
1 tablespoon vinegar
1 teaspoon salt
16-ounce can pork and beans
8½-ounce can lima beans
16-ounce can kidney beans

Preheat oven to 325 degrees. Sauté first 3 ingredients in skillet, stirring with a fork to break up the meat as it browns. Add the remaining ingredients and mix well. Bake in a 2-quart casserole for 2 hours at 325 degrees. Serves 6.

Chicken in the Woods

This is a favorite at our cottage. It goes well with a light-bodied red wine, or with beer.

2 frying chickens, cut up
2 cups wild rice
5 cups salt-free chicken stock
1 pound fresh mushrooms
4 tablespoons butter
Salt and pepper to taste

Start cooking the wild rice in the stock. Sprinkle the chicken pieces with salt and pepper and set in a casserole pan. Roast at 350 degrees for 50 minutes or until chicken is done. Sauté the mushrooms in the butter and set aside. When the chicken is done, remove it to a warm plate and cover with foil. Pour out the liquid from the casserole pan, degrease it, and mix it into the cooking rice. Keep an eye on the rice. The grains will begin to open at one hour. They will continue to open and the rice should be fully cooked in 1½ hours. When it is done, add salt and pepper to taste. Mix the mushrooms into the rice. Cover the bottom of the casserole with a bit of the rice and then add the chicken pieces. Put the rest of the rice in amidst the chicken. Serves 6. —*John Minnich*

Italian Chicken

You can get this ready for the oven in the morning, refrigerate, and enjoy predinner cocktails with your company while it bakes in the oven! The Italians love this dish, and there's no reason you won't like it, too. (For Norwegians and Swedes, better leave out the garlic.)

    2 fryer chickens, cut up
    1 cup butter
    1 cup grated Parmesan cheese
    2 cups Italian bread crumbs
    ¼ teaspoon minced garlic
    Salt to taste
    Parsley flakes

Skin chicken pieces if desired. Melt butter in baking pan. Combine cheese, bread crumbs, garlic, salt, and parsley flakes. Dip chicken pieces in butter and roll in crumb mixture. Arrange in pan and bake, uncovered, 1 hour at 375 degrees. You can bake potatoes in oven with chicken and serve with fresh vegetables of the season. Serves 8.

Baked Chicken

A super-easy recipe to feed the whole gang.

    2 pounds cut-up chicken
    1 teaspoon seasoning salt
    Black pepper to taste

¾ cup melted butter
3 cups bread crumbs or crushed cornflakes

Sprinkle the salt and pepper over chicken pieces. Dip each piece in butter, then roll in bread crumbs and set them in a baking pan. Cover and bake for 30 minutes at 350 degrees. Reduce oven to 250, baste chicken pieces with the remaining butter, and bake for 1 hour. Serves 4–6.

Barbecued Chicken in the Oven

Another chicken recipe, but a little more work. Is the company worth it?

½ cup bread crumbs
1 teaspoon brown sugar
1 teaspoon chili powder
½ teaspoon garlic powder
¼ teaspoon dry mustard
¼ teaspoon paprika
¼ teaspoon celery seed
3 pounds chicken parts
Salt and pepper
¼ cup butter, melted

Preheat oven to 375 degrees. Combine first 7 ingredients to make crumb mixture. Rinse chicken parts, pat dry with paper towels, and season with salt and pepper. Brush each chicken part with melted butter and roll in crumb mixture. Place parts in shallow baking pan, skin side up. Don't crowd. Bake at 375 degrees 50 minutes or until tender, and do not turn pieces, ever, ever, ever. Serves 8 hungry people, 6 ravenous people.

Tim's Sunday Chicken

Here's a good and easy recipe contributed by Tim Lloyd, chef extraordinaire at Monty's Blue Plate Diner, in Madison, Wisconsin.

1 cut-up fryer (2 thighs, 2 breasts, 2 legs, 2 wings)
2–3 large potatoes, cut into 1/8-inch slices
4 carrots, cut into 1/4-inch coins
1 onion, coarsely chopped
1/2 cup soy sauce
1–2 tablespoons garlic powder, according to taste
1–2 tablespoons dried parsley

Place chicken into 9x12-inch baking dish. Arrange vegetables among and around chicken pieces. Sprinkle with soy sauce, then sprinkle seasonings on top. Bake 1 hour at 400 degrees. Serves 3–4. *—Tim Lloyd*

Lemon Chicken

A nice recipe, and it takes only 15 minutes to make.

4 six-ounce boneless, skinless chicken breasts
1 tablespoon olive oil
2 tablespoons lemon juice
1 teaspoon sugar
Salt and pepper to taste
1/4 cup fresh Italian (flat-leafed) parsley, chopped

Place the chicken breasts between two pieces of wax paper and whack them with a large, heavy skillet until they are a quarter-inch thick. In same skillet, heat the olive oil and brown the chicken 2 minutes on each side. (That's 4 minutes—put away the calculator.) Set aside. Add lemon juice and 2 tablespoons of water to the skillet. Simmer to reduce the liquid by half, then add the sugar, salt, and pepper to taste. Spoon sauce over chicken and garnish with parsley before serving. Serve with rice or pasta and salad. Serves 4.

Chicken Picante

Nothing zips up a chicken like this Southwestern recipe using picante sauce. Some say it was discovered in Texas, others swear it was invented in New Mexico, or even south of the border. Actually, it was discovered on the back of a jar of picante sauce.

1½ cups picante sauce (medium or hot)
3 tablespoons packed brown sugar
1 tablespoon mustard (preferably Dijon)
4 boneless, skinless chicken breasts
3 cups cooked rice or pasta

Preheat oven to 400 degrees. Mix the picante sauce with the sugar and mustard. Place chicken in a 2-quart shallow baking dish (do not crowd). Pour sauce over chicken and bake at 400 degrees for 20 minutes or until chicken is done. Serve with rice or pasta. Serves 4.

Chicken Casserole

This is quick and easy, maybe even impressive.

14½-ounce can stewed tomatoes
2 cans cream of celery soup
16-ounce can French-cut green beans, drained
3 cups chicken, cooked and diced
1½ teaspoons Italian seasoning
2 cups Bisquick
1½ cups milk
½ cup cheddar cheese, shredded

Preheat oven to 450 degrees. Mix tomatoes, soup, beans, chicken, and 1 teaspoon Italian seasoning in ungreased 13x9x2-inch pan. Beat together Bisquick and milk. Pour evenly over chicken mixture. Sprinkle with cheese and ½ teaspoon of Italian seasoning. Bake 25 to 27 minutes or until crust is light golden brown and cheese is melted. Serves 6.

Ridiculously Easy Chicken Pot Pie

1½ cups frozen peas and carrots
2 cups cooked, diced chicken
¼ cup chopped mushrooms
¼ cup chopped onion
4 eggs
1⅓ cups milk
¾ cup Bisquick
½ teaspoon salt
Dash of pepper

Thaw and drain the peas and carrots. Heat oven to 400 degrees. Grease a 10-inch pie plate. Mix chicken, peas, carrots, mushrooms, and onions in the pie plate. Beat the eggs, milk, Bisquick, salt, and pepper until smooth, then pour over the chicken mixture in the pie plate. Bake 30–35 minutes, until a table knife inserted into the center comes out clean. Serves 6.

Chicken-Mushroom Linguini in Cream Sauce
More fun with mushroom soup!

4 tablespoons olive oil
1 medium onion, sliced
6 cloves garlic, minced
2 small cans mushroom pieces
4 chicken breasts, cut into strips
2 cans cream of mushroom soup
1 cup dry white wine
1 pound uncooked linguini

Set the water to boil for the linguini. In a large skillet, in olive oil, saute the onion, garlic, mushrooms, and chicken strips until chicken is no longer pink inside. Add soup and wine and simmer approximately 20 minutes. Cook the linguini at the same time. Serve chicken mixture over linguini. Serves 6.

Fettucine Carbonara

An Italian classic—and easy as pizza! (Easy as pie, you say? Well, "pizza" is the Italian word for "pie," so saying "Easy as pizza" is the same as saying "Easy as pie." It's sort of a bilingual play on words, you see, and—oh, forget it.)

4 eggs
1/4 cup heavy cream
1/2 pound bacon or pancetta, cut into 1-inch sections
4 ounce button mushrooms, sliced
1 pound uncooked fettucine or tagliatelle
1/4 cup butter or oleo
1 cup grated Parmasan or Romano cheese
1/3 cup snipped parsley
Pepper to taste (preferably white pepper)

Bring the eggs, butter, and cream to room temperature. Put a serving dish into the oven and heat to 250 degrees. Cook the bacon pieces with mushrooms until brown, then drain on paper towels. Cook pasta in boiling water till al dente (10–12 minutes) and drain. While it is boiling, mix together the eggs and cream. Put cooked pasta into hot serving dish and toss with butter. Pour the egg-cream mixture over pasta and toss well. Add bacon, mushrooms, cheese, and parsley and toss again. Season with pepper and serve immediately. Serves 6 as a main dish, 10 as a side dish.

Wild Mushroom Fettucine

If you have found some wild mushrooms, eaten them, and haven't died, you might try this recipe. It's really good. (Seriously—don't eat wild mushrooms unless you're certain of what you're eating.)

1 pound dry fettucine
2 cloves garlic, minced
1 large onion, chopped
4 to 6 cups wild mushrooms
4 plum tomatoes seeded and chopped
Salt and pepper
1 teaspoon dried rosemary
1 cup chicken broth
1 cup heavy cream
2 splashes Madeira or sherry

First, start the fettucine in boiling water. Immediately saute the garlic and onion slightly in butter, then add mushrooms and cook just a little while longer. Add the chopped tomatoes and continue to cook. Add salt and pepper to taste. Add the rosemary, chicken broth, and cream, and cook until the sauce thickens. Add the wine. Serve over drained fettucine. Serves 6.

Fettucine Alfredo

Often, the best recipes are the simplest. Here is a classic Roman recipe using only four ingredients, plus a dash of pepper. Of course, the success of the dish depends on the freshness and quality of the ingredients. Some cooks insist on tampering with this classic dish by adding things such as ham and peas. Resist the temptation. I must admit, however, that I do add just the smallest pinch of nutmeg to the sauce, and I love it that way. (Note: This isn't exactly the best recipe for cholesterol-watchers.)

1 pound fettuccine
½ cup butter
⅔ cup heavy cream
1¼ cup fresh grated Parmesan cheese
Dash of pepper

Cook fettuccine according to directions. Drain and keep warm while you prepare the sauce. Heat the butter and cream in a saucepan until the butter has melted. Remove from heat, add 1 cup of the Parmesan and the pepper. Stir until the sauce is blended and smooth. Pour sauce over the fettuccine, toss gently until pasta is coated, and serve immediately. Allow guests to sprinkle more Parmesan on top, if they wish. Serves 4.

Eggplant Parmesan

Fettuccine Alfredo is a good dish to serve when vegetarians come over for dinner. Here's another veggie favorite that's easy to prepare and that all will enjoy.

1 large eggplant
2 eggs
¼ cup water
2 cups breadcrumbs (Italian or plain)

1 tablespoon dried oregano
1 tablespoon dried basil
Salt and pepper to taste
¼ cup parmesan cheese, grated
8 ounces mozzarella cheese, grated
1 jar of your favorite spaghetti or marinara sauce
(see following recipe)

Preheat the oven to 350 degrees. Peel the eggplant, cut it in ¼-inch slices, and drain slices on paper toweling. Beat eggs with the water. In a separate bowl, mix together the breadcrumbs, oregano, basil, salt and pepper, and cheeses. Dip each eggplant slice in egg, coat with the breadcrumb mixture, layer them in a baking dish, and cover them with spaghetti sauce. Bake, uncovered, in a 350-degree oven for 30–40 minutes, until sauce is bubbling. Serves 4.

Spaghetti with Marinara Sauce

This easy recipe will please the whole crowd. It doesn't call for meatballs, but of course you can add them to the sauce if you wish. Many groceries also have frozen precooked Italian sausage that you can add to the sauce.

1 teaspoon grated garlic
½ cup olive oil
28-ounce can crushed Italian flavored tomatoes
½ teaspoon ground thyme
1 ounce sherry or red wine
Salt and pepper to taste
1 pound pasta (any variety)
3 ounces grated Asiago or Parmesan cheese

Place garlic in frying pan with heated olive oil and simmer until tender. Add the tomatoes, thyme, sherry, and salt and pepper and simmer for 10 minutes. Meanwhile, start to boil 4 quarts of water; when it comes to a rolling boil, add the pasta and cook until al dente. Drain the pasta until no more water drips from it. Serve pasta immediately, topped with marinara sauce and sprinkled with grated cheese. Serves 4. —*James Novak*

Creamy Pork Chops

More fun with mushroom soup—and only 20 minutes start to finish!

Wild rice mix
1½ tablespoons cooking oil
4 boneless pork chops, ¾-inch thick
1 can condensed cream of mushroom soup
½ can milk (use same soup can)
Paprika

Put rice on to boil, following directions on box. Heat oil in skillet. Add chops and brown. Mix soup and milk and add to chops. Heat to boil, then cover and cook under low heat 10–12 minutes. Spoon liquid over chops, sprinkle with paprika, and serve with rice and vegetable of choice. Serves 4.

Ham Steak with Apples

How to use those fresh apples from the roadside stand with that leftover ham in the fridge.

3 teaspoons butter
¼ cup firmly packed brown sugar
2 tablespoons mustard (preferably Dijon)
2 cups cored apples, unpeeled and sliced across into rounds
1 pound precooked ham steak

In heavy skillet melt butter until bubbling. Stir in brown sugar and mustard. Add apples. Cook over medium heat, stirring occasionally, until apples are semitender (5–7 minutes). Place ham steak in same skillet and place apple rounds on top of steak. Cover and cook 5–7 minutes, until ham is heated through. Serves 2–3.

Slow Cooked Boston Butt

Here's another recipe contributed by chef Tim Lloyd. It's ridiculously easy and will fill the cottage with the most delicious aroma for the whole afternoon.

1 Boston butt pork roast (4–5 pounds, boneless)
2 cups apple juice
½ cup soy sauce

Place roast in shallow baking pan, cover with liquids, and bake uncovered for 6 hours at 250 degrees. Awesome! —*Tim Lloyd*

Ham and Pea Soup

Here's another reason you'll be glad you have that leftover ham.

10 cups water
2 cups dried split peas, yellow or green
3/4 pound of cooked ham, cubed
2 bay leaves
1/2 teaspoon dried thyme
1/2 teaspoon dried marjoram
2 medium onions, minced
2 carrots, peeled and sliced
Salt and pepper to taste

Rinse the peas and put them into the water. Add the ham and seasonings and bring to a boil. Reduce heat, cover, and simmer for 2 hours. Then add the onions and carrots and continue simmering for another 30 minutes or until peas are tender. Adjust seasonings, remove bay leaves, and serve with good European-style bread. Serves 4.

Caroline's Turkey Patties

1/2 pound dumpling egg noodles
1 medium onion, chopped
1 egg
5 tablespoons milk
1 package (1 1/4 pound) ground Jennie-O turkey
1/4 cup unseasoned breadcrumbs
1 1/2 teaspoon seasoned salt
1/2 teaspoon dry thyme
1/4 teaspoon dillweed
Cooking oil
2 medium tomatoes, cut into wedges
Garlic

Put dumpling egg noodles on to boil. Sauté onion until soft but not burned. Set aside. In mixing bowl, beat eggs and milk. Add turkey, breadcrumbs, sautéed onion, and seasonings and mix well. Shape mixture into small patties (about 2½ inches in diameter) and brown on both sides in oiled skillet. When all patties are browned, wipe out pan with paper towel and add just enough water to cover bottom of pan. Return patties to pan, cover, reduce heat, and simmer until patties are no longer pink inside. Remove patties and keep warm. Sauté tomato wedges, serve with turkey patties over cooked noodles. Serves 4. —*Caroline Erickson*

Ellen's Kohlrouladen (Stuffed Cabbage)

I met Ellen Zybill in the 1980s, when she was a graduate student at the University of Wisconsin-Madison. Ellen was a good cook, and she made these kohlrouladens for us one night. My grandmother used to make them, too—but used pork instead of beef and called them "pigs in blankets." Maybe these are cows in blankets. Whatever they are, you'll like them.

    1 medium head green cabbage
    1 pound ground beef
    1 egg
    1 medium chopped onion
    2 tablespoons breadcrumbs
    Salt and pepper to taste
    1 tablespoon chopped parsley
    4 tablespoons tomato paste

Cook whole head of cabbage for 8 minutes in boiling water. Cool, then separate the leaves and fill each of them with the mixture of beef, egg, onion, breadcrumbs, salt, pepper, and parsley. Form rolls, tuck in ends, and place tightly in pot (so they do not unfold). Cover with boiling water. Simmer for 45 minutes. Mix tomato paste with pot water to make a sauce to pour over the cabbage rolls. Serves 4. —*Ellen Zybill*

Pork Fajitas

Olé! Make mine Mexican tonight!

    1½ pounds boneless, lean pork loin
    1 clove garlic

2 tablespoons orange juice
2 tablespoons cider vinegar
½ teaspoon oregano
½ teaspoon thyme
1 teaspoon cumin
1 teaspoon chili powder
1 teaspoon adobo seasoning (if available)
1 teaspoon seasoned salt
¼ cup cooking oil
1 medium onion, diced
1 medium green pepper, diced
1 stalk celery, diced
Tortillas
Hot salsa

Rub pork with garlic. Cut into thin strips. In a large skillet over medium heat, combine the orange juice, vinegar, and seasonings. Drizzle in the cooking oil. Add the pork and toss well. Add the onion, green pepper, and celery, and cook until pork and vegetables are tender, about 15 minutes. Meanwhile, warm the tortillas in the oven at 250 degrees. Spoon mixture into warm tortillas, roll up, and serve with hot salsa. Good served with canned refried beans and Mexican rice. Serves 4.

Weiner Schnitzel

This traditional German dish is easier than you think, and better than you remember. The Germans would put a fried egg on top of each steak before serving.

2 pounds veal steak
Salt and pepper
Cracker or bread crumbs
2 eggs, beaten
Cooking oil
Lemon juice

Cut the veal into ½-inch-thick steaks. Sprinkle with salt and pepper. Dip in cracker or bread crumbs, then in beaten egg, then again in crumbs. Let stand a few minutes and then fry on both sides in oil. Dry on paper towel, sprinkle with lemon juice, and serve. Serves 4–6.

Baked Spare Ribs with Sauerkraut and Dumplings

This is a great recipe for a chilly autumn night. From my old Pennsylvania Dutch cookbook.

4 pounds pork spare ribs
14-ounce can sauerkraut
2 cups flour
1 egg, beaten
1 teaspoon baking powder
1 cup whole milk

Cut the spare ribs into serving portions and arrange in the bottom of a roasting pan. Add the sauerkraut, cover the pan, and bake in a moderate oven (350 degrees) for 1½ hours. Make dumplings by combining the flour, baking powder, milk, and egg. Drop by spoonfuls on the sauerkraut. Cover pan tightly and finish baking for 30 more minutes. Serves 4.

WE KILLED IT.

Let's Eat It!

WHEN WE'RE UP NORTH, we occasionally can't resist examining the wildlife up close — by shooting it or hooking it on a line. When this urge takes hold, and we are successful in satisfying that ancient hunting lust that lies deep within us, we must think of something to do with the quarry. Ergo, here are a few recipes for fur, feather, and fin. (Well, actually those are the parts we won't be eating — but you get the idea.)

North Woods Braised Rabbit

This recipe is great with roasted root vegetables, salad, and bread for sopping up the gravy. It also lends itself to crockpot cooking. Just pre-pare, on stovetop, through the point where everything is mixed together. Then throw it into the crockpot, set the temperature, and go fishing—or go out and bag some more bunnies.

2½- to 3-pound rabbit, cut into serving-sized pieces
Salt and pepper to taste
3 tablespoons cooking oil
½ cup Dijon mustard
1 tablespoon butter
1 bottle inexpensive dry white wine
1 medium onion, diced
1 tablespoon all-purpose flour
1 teaspoon thyme
1 bay leaf

Brush meat with mustard, season with salt and pepper, and brown in oil in a heavy-bottomed skillet or Dutch oven (the Lodge cast iron pans work well). Remove rabbit and deglaze pan with ⅓ cup of the wine. Add the onion and cook until translucent. Add flour to pan, stirring out any lumps, and pour in the remaining wine, the thyme, and bay leaf. Add meat, cover, and simmer slowly until the meat is fork-tender and the sauce thickens. Serves 6–8. —*Mary Lorenzen*

Deer Camp Venison Stew

Here is a great guy recipe. (Aye, but the ladies like it, too!) Anybody who plans to bag a buck will be sure to have the proper spices in store.

5 pounds venison, cut into ¾-inch cubes
All-purpose flour
Seasoning salt
5 quarts beef broth
1½ cups brewed coffee
½ cup catsup
2 medium onions, diced
½ teaspoon thyme
½ teaspoon garlic powder
¼ teaspoon black pepper

Salt to taste
1 teaspoon celery salt
1 teaspoon chili powder
½ teaspoon sweet basil
8 potatoes, cut into 1-inch cubes
8 carrots, sliced into discs
1 pound frozen peas
Butter

Dust venison with flour and seasoning salt. Brown in a large roasting pan or Dutch oven. Add the beef broth, coffee, catsup, onions, and all the seasonings. Bring to a boil, then reduce heat and simmer for 2 hours or until venison is tender. Add the potatoes and carrots and simmer until tender. Add more liquid if necessary to keep the venison and vegetables covered. Add the frozen peas last. Thicken as desired with a roux made by mixing equal parts softened butter and flour. May be served over biscuits, if desired. Serves 10–12.

Stokes' No-Sweat Venison Roast

Bill Stokes is a legendary outdoorsman, angler, and hunter, renowned columnist for the Chicago Tribune, Milwaukee Journal, and Wisconsin State Journal, and an all-around swell guy. I don't think he's ever actually shot a deer, unless by accident, but nevertheless he has kindly consented to share his venison roast recipe with us. Here it is, in Bill's own inimitable words.

Shoot a deer. Put a large roast, or three small ones, in a roasting pan. Sprinkle generously with salt, pepper, sage, and thyme. Place thick slices of onion on top of roast, and tuck some whole onions in around the roast. Pour two cans of cream of mushroom soup over the roasts, and add two cans of water—which prevents things from drying out in case you have to track a wounded deer and don't get back to the cabin when you expect to. Throw in several bay leaves. Cover, place in oven at 300–350, and get the hell out of the cabin where everyone else is already having fun.

There was never any set time for how long to roast this concoction. It depended on what was going on out in the woods or along the creek. If I happened back to the cabin at some point, I would sometimes pour some red wine over the roast. An hour or so before you are to eat, add carrots and potatoes—never peel them because that is boring and takes too much time. Place back in the oven until spuds are done.

Put the roasting pan on a trivet in the middle of a large table with a serving spoon and fork. Set out plates, maybe a bowl of cranberries and a jug of red wine, and stand back! Sometimes if it worked out I would get up to the spring pond for some watercress and there would be a salad, but only if it didn't interfere with recreational pursuits. Like all "cooks" I expected and appreciated compliments from the lip-smackers, and later if they allowed me one extra story around the campfire, maybe it was because of the no-sweat roast. Cheers. *—Bill Stokes*

Baked Pheasant

My recipe file has this marked as "Governor's Mansion." Don't know much more, and neither did the Governor's Mansion.

    1 pheasant
    1½ teaspoons salt
    ½ teaspoon pepper
    ½ teaspoon Accent (MSG)
    ½ pound butter
    1 cup cooking sherry
    2 tablespoons lemon juice
    2 tablespoons sugar
    1 can condensed cream of mushroom soup
    1 can condensed cream of chicken soup

Clean and dress the bird. Cut into serving pieces and rinse. Sprinkle with salt, pepper, and Accent, then brown in a deep skillet in butter. Transfer to a roasting pan. Combine the sherry, lemon juice, honey, and soups, mixing well. Pour this over the pheasant and bake in a moderate oven (350 degrees) for about 2 hours. Serves 4.

Orange Wild Duck

Steve Miller, originally from De Pere, now of Madison, is a lifetime duck hunter. Here is his longtime favorite recipe for all wild ducks, from mallards to the stronger-tasting divers such as goldeneye and bufflehead.

    1 large wild duck or 2 small ducks, cut into serving-size pieces
    2 tablespoons butter
    2 tablespoons virgin olive oil

6-ounce can orange juice concentrate (or equivalent orange juice)
1/4 cup water
1/2 teaspoon caraway seed
Salt and pepper to taste

Heat butter with olive oil in a heavy metal skillet. Brown all pieces of duck. Add orange juice, water, and caraway seed. Cover and simmer gently until duck pieces are tender. Add olive oil and water as needed for moisture. Simmer about 60–90 minutes. Add salt and pepper while duck is simmering. Serve with cranberry sauce, good bread or biscuits, and wild rice or potatoes. —*Steve Miller*

Orange Duck Soup

Here's a good way to use up excess fowl, if yesterday's hunt was more than successful. If you have some leftover cooked wild rice, as well, it wouldn't hurt to throw that into the recipe.

3 tablespoons onion, chopped fine
3 tablespoons butter
6 cups beef or chicken broth
1 cup peeled and diced carrots
1/2 cup green peas
2 1/2 cups cooked duck meat, cubed
1 cup orange juice
1 cup cooked wild rice (optional)
2 tablespoons cornstarch
Salt and pepper to taste

In a large soup pot, sauté the onions in butter until soft but not burned. Add the broth, carrots, peas, and duck meat. Bring to a boil, then reduce heat and simmer for 20 minutes. Add the orange juice and wild rice (if on hand) and continue simmering for another 20 minutes. In a small bowl or custard cup, dissolve the cornstarch in a half-cup of water. Add to the soup and stir constantly while the soup thickens. Adjust seasoning with salt and pepper. Serves 4.

Basic Fried Bluegills

Quick and easy.

   2 pounds bluegill, cleaned
   Garlic salt to taste
   Black pepper to taste
   Cooking oil
   Yellow cornmeal

Mix all ingredients in sealed plastic bag, turning and shaking gently until all bluegill pieces are well covered. Fry in hot oil 3 minutes or until done. Drain on paper towels. Serves 4–6.

Lemon-Fried Bluegills

Takes a little longer, but adds a tangy zest to bluegill.

   2 pounds bluegill, cleaned
   1 cup all-purpose flour
   ½ teaspoon salt
   2 teaspoons grated lemon peel
   1 cup water
   Cooking oil

Mix flour, salt, lemon peel, and water. Fry in hot oil 3 minutes or until done. Drain on paper towels. Serves 4–6.

North Woods No-Shrimp Cocktail

We don' need no stinking shrimp—we got fish!

Boil whole bluegill or other small lake fish in boiling water for 6 minutes (or sliced fillets of a larger fish) until flesh turns opaque. Do not overcook. Remove from water and, with a fork, remove chunks of meat from the bones. Chill well, and serve with cocktail sauce.

Nut-Fried, Double-Dipped Walleye

Here is a recipe from my favorite Wisconsin game warden, an experienced and accomplished outdoorsman and photographer, and author of the popular book, *Wisconsin Waterfalls*. If anybody knows how to skin a walleye, it's Pat Lisi.

3 pounds freshly caught walleyes, skinned and filleted
1 cup all-purpose flour
1 tablespoon seasoning (I sure like Emeril's Essence)
Pepper to taste
1 cup pistachio nuts, finely chopped
¼ cup pine nuts, finely chopped
3 eggs
1 cup buttermilk
1 cup vegetable oil
Salt to taste

Heat oil in pan to 350–370 degrees. Mix seasonings with the flour. Mix buttermilk and eggs. Mix nuts together in a separate bowl. Bathe walleye fillets one at a time in buttermilk/egg mixture, let excess drip completely off each fillet, then dredge on both sides with flour/seasoning mixture. Put fillet back into buttermilk, let all excess drip off again, then cover with nut mixture. Prepare all the fillets in this manner. When oil is hot, carefully lay fillets in pan. Cook both sides to brown (don't overcook!), approximately 4–5 minutes each side. When finished, remove from pan and immediately add the salt to taste. Serves 6. *–Pat Lisi*

Garlic Fried Walleye

2 pounds walleye fillets
1 teaspoon salt
Dash of pepper
½ teaspoon Old Bay Seasoning
2 eggs
1 cup all-purpose flour
1 cup cracker crumbs
Olive oil
¼ pound butter, melted
3 cloves garlic, minced

Sprinkle fish with salt and pepper, and dredge in flour mixed with Old Bay Seasoning. Beat the eggs and put them in a shallow dish. Dip each fillet in egg, then roll in crumbs. Heat the oil in a heavy skillet and fry until the fish is golden brown and the flesh is flaky white. Remove to a warm platter. Place the melted butter in the hot skillet, add the minced garlic, and cook until the butter just turns brown. Pour over the fish. Serves 6.

Fried Smallmouth Bass

This recipe will serve two people, but may be doubled or even tripled for a larger party, provided that you are a competent bass angler.

> 1 pound smallmouth bass fillets
> 1 stick butter
> 2/3 cup yellow cornmeal
> 2/3 cup flour
> 2 tablespoons vinegar
> Salt and pepper to taste
> Paprika

Mix cornmeal, flour, salt, and pepper with fillets in sealable plastic bag. Fry in melted butter over medium heat until browned on both sides. Drain on paper towels. Add vinegar to butter in pan and pour over fish before serving. Sprinkle with paprika. Serves 2. (May be served with tartar sauce, for which see recipe on page 87.)

Easy Deep-Fried Bass

The quantities are up to you. How many bass did you land today?

Mix yellow cornmeal, salt, pepper, and bass fillets in sealable plastic bag. Turn to coat fillets thoroughly. Fry in hot cooking oil in a deep cast iron pot or Dutch oven (or an outdoor fish cooker) until golden brown. Serve with store-bought potato salad, vegetable of choice, and plenty of cold beer.

Tangy Salmon on the Grill

The following two recipes are for the grill—but, for campers, they work equally well over an open fire, provided a cooking grate can be suspended 6–7 inches above coals.

> 1 salmon fillet, 3–4 pounds, ½-inch thick
> 1½ tablespoons honey
> Kosher salt
> Freshly ground black pepper
> Chili powder
> 1 lime, quartered

Start the grill and bring charcoal up to cooking temperature. Place salmon fillet, skin side down, on an ungreased piece of aluminum foil. Pat the fillet dry with a paper towel. Lightly drizzle honey along the fillet and rub it into the flesh with your fingers. Sprinkle the fillet with a little kosher salt, ground pepper, and chili powder. I never measure these, but just put on a light coating of each. Squeeze the juice from one-quarter lime over the fish. Place on the grill, lower the cover, and cook about 12–13 minutes without lifting the cover or flipping the fish. It's done when it feels slightly firm when touched near the center of the fillet. Remove the fish from the grill and lightly score into 6–7 servings. The skin will stick to the foil and a spatula carefully slipped just under the meat will free the skin from the fillet. Squeeze remaining lime wedges over the fish just before serving. Serves 6.

Wonderful Grilled Whitefish

The salmon recipe, above, works equally as well for whitefish fillets—but eliminate the honey and substitute paprika for chili powder. You will have beautiful whole fillets for the platter. —*Larry Sperling*

Fried Smelts

Oh m'gawd, they brought home a mess o' smelts. Now what? Well, it's time for a good old-fashioned smelt fry. Here's how.

Clean and rinse the fish, remove the heads and backbones if you want, pat them dry with paper towels, and keep them iced until ready to cook. For each dozen smelt, get out two eggs. Coat the fish lightly with flour. Lightly beat the eggs and dip each smelt into egg, then coat it with flour seasoned with salt, pepper, Old Bay Seasoning, and cayenne to taste. Fry them, a few at a time, in deep fat (370 degrees) for 3–5 minutes or until golden brown. Drain them on paper towels and keep them in a warming oven until all are ready to serve.

If you want to be fancy, serve the smelt with the following remoulade sauce.

To 1½ cups mayonnaise add 1 medium onion, 2 anchovies, and 1 dill pickle, all finely chopped, 1 tablespoon each of capers, parsley, tarragon, and chervil, all chopped, and 1 teaspoon mustard. Thin the sauce with cream and season with ½ teaspoon each of lemon juice and sugar, and salt and pepper to taste. (If you don't want to be fancy, just mix mustard, mayonnaise, and minced onion. Or, mix 1½ cups of bottled chili sauce with 3 tablespoons of prepared horseradish.)

Cleaning smelt: To clean smelt, snip off the heads, removing the pectoral fins. Insert a knife into the rear of the fish and cut along the belly to the point where you cut off the head. With finger or spoon, remove entrails, starting at the back and working forward. For large smelt, you may also want to remove the backbone. With a knife, working inside the body cavity, make a cut on both sides of the backbone, cutting through the ribs. Then grab the backbone at tail end and pull it out from the inside, leaving the soft rib bones.

Barbecued Trout

Freshly caught trout
Fresh lemon or lime
½ cup soy sauce
½ cup cooking sherry
¼ cup cooking oil
1 clove garlic, minced

Clean fish, rinse, brush inside and out with fresh lemon or lime juice, and place in a shallow pan. Mix together the soy sauce, sherry, cooking oil, and garlic, and pour this marinade over fish. Let stand one hour. Fish may then be barbecued over coals, 10–15 minutes, depending on size of fish. May also be fried indoors in a skillet. Baste with the marinade.

Lemon-butter sauce for fish: Melt ¼ cup butter with 2 tablespoons lemon juice and serve hot with fish.

Buttered Baked Trout

This works well for trout, but actually is good for nearly any fish. The amounts of seasoning you use depend on how much fish you have.

> Freshly caught trout (or fillet of larger fish)
> Garlic salt
> Old Bay Seasoning
> Seasoned salt
> Lemon pepper
> Chopped onions
> Butter

Mix together the dry seasonings, then mix them with the chopped onions. Coat the fish well with this mixture. Encase each trout or fillet in aluminum foil, pat with butter, and close foil tightly. Bake in oven for 30–40 minutes at 400 degrees, or on outdoor grill.

Herbed Lake Perch

> 2 pounds fresh lake perch fillets
> 1 cup all-purpose flour
> Salt and pepper to taste
> 4 teaspoons paprika
> 2 teaspoons dry rosemary
> 1 teaspoon dry oregano
> 4 eggs
> 3 cups bread crumbs
> 6 tablespoons butter
> ½ cup vegetable oil
> Lemon wedges

Mix together the flour, salt, pepper, paprika, and rosemary. Beat the eggs in a bowl. Dip each fillet in egg, then roll in the crumb mixture. Melt the butter with the oil in a deep skillet and fry the fillets a few at a time until golden brown—no more than a minute in the pan. Drain finished fillets on paper towels and keep in a warm oven until all are done and ready to serve. Serve with lemon wedges. Tartar sauce is optional. Serves 4.

Oven Fried Catfish

Here's a recipe I got from an old towboat captain when I tied up my raft one stormy night on a sandbar outside Winona, Minnesota . . . OK, I really found it stuffed into my recipe file and I don't know where it came from. But it's a good one. If you got yourself a mess o' catfish, you're in for some good eatin' with this recipe.

>   2 tablespoons lemon juice
>   2 tablespoons white wine
>   ½ cup bread crumbs
>   Dash salt
>   Dash pepper
>   Dash garlic powder
>   1 pound catfish fillets
>   1 tablespoon olive oil
>   Tartar sauce
>   Lemon wedges

Preheat the oven to 450 degrees. Grease a large, shallow baking pan. In a bowl, combine the lemon juice and wine. In a separate bowl, mix together the bread crumbs, salt, pepper, and garlic powder. Dip each fillet in the liquid, then coat with the crumbs. Arrange fillets, one deep, in the big pan and drizzle with oil. Bake at 450 degrees for 10–12 minutes, or until flesh is flaky. Serve with tartar sauce and lemon wedges. Serves 2–3.

Catfish Tomato Stew

This is a recipe a friend from North Carolina sent to me, some years ago. If some of the anglers in the crowd come home with some fresh catfish, here's a good way to use a couple of them.

>   ½ pound bacon, diced
>   1½ pounds onions, chopped
>   2 cans condensed cream of tomato soup
>   1½ pints water

2 pounds dressed catfish fillets, backbones removed
Salt and pepper to taste
²⁄₃ bottle catsup

Fry bacon until crisp. Drain off fat. Cook onions in bacon fat until lightly browned. Add soup and water and bring to a boil. Dice catfish and add in. Simmer for 20 minutes. Add salt and pepper to taste. Add catsup and stir. Serves 6.

Pickled Fish

If you can't use all those fish that the guys brought back, talk them into having a pickling party. Here's an old Wisconsin recipe, good with almost any kind of meaty fish.

3 pounds whitefish, lake trout, bass, almost anything
1½ cups cider vinegar
1 teaspoon salt
½ cup sugar
1 jalapeno pepper, sliced and seeded (optional)
½ cup pickling spices
3 bay leaves

Clean and bone the fish and cut it into serving-size pieces. Put them in a cooking pot with the vinegar, salt, sugar, pepper, and pickling spices (the last of which should be tied into a little cheesecloth bag). Barely cover with water, bring to a boil, and simmer for 10–12 minutes. Let cool, then chill in refrigerator, covered with pickling liquid. For long-term use, place fish in sterile jars while still hot, cover with pickling liquid, and seal.

Norwegian Lutefisk

Lutefisk is dried lingcod that has been subjected to slaked lime and soda. Do not make lutefisk.

THE RAIN STOPPED.
Let's Cook Outside

ONE OF THE PLEASURES OF SUMMER cottage life is cooking on the old barbecue grill and eating outdoors. How better to enjoy nature's al fresco paradise—the breeze off the lake, the pine needles falling softly into the barbecue sauce, the clouds of greasy smoke rolling into your eyes, the playful nibble of giant mosquitoes? If you're an experienced cook, though, the best part about cooking outdoors is that you don't have to do it. There's always some guy—and it's always a guy—who is willing to don the apron, grab his man-sized tongs, fork, and spatula, and demonstrate full mastery over the Weber.

We bless these guys. They're part of what makes summer fun at the cottage. Just stand back fifty yards when he lights the grill.

Here are some recipes for the grill that go somewhat beyond the usual hot dogs, hamburgers, and brats.

Beef Kebabs

"Kebab" is Turkish for broiled meat. The old Turkish soldiers used to impale slabs of red meat on their swords and roast them over an open fire. Grrrr! We have refined the process, but the beef tastes just as good—maybe better.

> 2 pounds good-quality beefsteak
> 3/4 cup olive oil
> 6–8 bay leaves
> 4 medium green peppers, seeded and cut into squares
> 12 very small onions
> 12 cherry tomatoes

Cut steak into 1 1/2-inch cubes. Marinate them in oil with 5 or 6 bay leaves for 4–5 hours, turning occasionally. Thread the meat on skewers, alternating with green peppers, onion, and cherry tomatoes. Brush the meat and vegetables with the seasoned oil. Serve over rice or a wild rice mixture. Serves 6.

Seafood Kebabs

Sometimes the Turkish soldiers couldn't find animals to slay, and so they slew shrimps and scallops.

> 1/2 cup olive oil
> 1/4 cup lemon juice
> 1/4 teaspoon dried oregano
> 1/4 teaspoon dried thyme
> 1/4 teaspoon garlic powder
> Salt and pepper
> 2 tablespoons dry white wine
> 2 pounds raw scallops
> 2 pounds raw shrimp

Make a marinade of all ingredients except the scallops and shrimp. Mix well, pour over scallops and shrimp and marinate for 2–3 hours. Thread onto skewers or Turkish Army swords and grill over coals for 8–10 minutes, turning only once. Serve with rice or pasta and salad. Serves 6–8.

Salsa Steak Kebabs

These are good appetizers, or can serve as a main course. Great with beer. Start to marinate them in the morning so they'll be ready to grill by suppertime.

    1 cup salsa
    ¼ cup vegetable oil
    1½ teaspoon lemon pepper
    ½ teaspoon seasoned salt
    1 teaspoon garlic powder
    1½ pounds top sirloin steak, cut into ¾-inch cubes
    32 wooden skewers (4-inch)

Soak the wooden skewers in water, so they don't burn on the grill. Mix together the salsa, oil, and spices in a bowl. Marinate the beef cubes in the sauce for 2–6 hours, in the refrigerator. (You can use a large plastic bag for this.) Thread 2 beef cubes onto each skewer and grill over medium coals for 5–7 minutes, turning occasionally.

Wisconsin Brats

You thought brats were good before? Wait till you try this recipe!

    12 brats
    ½ stick butter
    Enough cheap beer to cover brats in pot
    2 green peppers, sliced
    2 medium onions, sliced
    12 brat buns

Put all ingredients in cooking pot. Bring to a boil and simmer 20 minutes. Brown the brats on the grill, then return to pot to keep them warm. When ready to serve, just shake off the beer and plop them back on the grill for 30 seconds. The cooked green peppers and onions are great when served on top of the brats, in buns.

(Note: I like brats cooked the way they used to do it at the Brat Haus, in Madison, Wisconsin. Slice the boiled brat down the middle, the long way, spread it out, and grill it first on the flat, cut side, then, flipped, on the rounded side. These brats have a crispy, smoky essence, and they lose a lot of fat in the process.)

Not the Same Old Hamburgers

Tired of the same old boring hamburgers? No, I didn't think you were. But try the following three Texas-style variations anyway. They're all good, and they all come directly from the Texas Beef Council. Don't mess with Texas.

Grilled Jalapeno Cheeseburgers

1 pound lean ground beef
2 teaspoons fresh jalapeno pepper, seeded and chopped
1½ teaspoons chili powder
¼ cup shredded Monterey Jack cheese
4 thin tomato slices
4 hamburger buns, split and toasted

In medium bowl, combine ground beef, jalapeno pepper, and chili powder, mixing lightly but thoroughly. Shape beef mixture into 4 patties, each ½-inch thick. Place patties on grid over medium-ash-covered coals. Grill uncovered 14–16 minutes or until centers are no longer pink, turning once. Check with a meat thermometer for an internal temperature of 160 degrees. Approximately one minute before burgers are done, sprinkle each with 1 tablespoon of cheese. Place one slice of tomato on bottom half of each bun and top with burger. Close sandwiches and serve. Serves 4.

Brew Burgers

1 1/2 pounds ground beef
1/4 cup beer
1/4 cup bottled steak sauce
4 slices sweet onion
4 slices (1 ounce each) Swiss cheese
4 crusty rolls, split
Salt
Lettuce leaves

Combine beer and steak sauce in a 1-cup glass measuring cup. Cover and microwave on high 1 to 1 1/2 minutes or until bubbly. Lightly shape ground beef into 4 patties, each 3/4-inch thick. Place patties in center of grid over medium-ash-covered coals; arrange onion slices around patties. Grill, uncovered, 13–15 minutes to 160-degree internal temperature. Season with salt after turning. About 2 minutes before patties are done, brush generously with sauce; top with cheese. Serve burgers and onions on rolls with lettuce and sauce. Serves 4.

Firecracker Burgers with Cooling Lime Sauce

1 1/2 pounds ground beef chuck
4 sesame seed sandwich rolls, split and toasted
1 cup watercress or mixed spring greens

Seasoning
1 tablespoon curry powder
1 tablespoon Caribbean jerk seasoning
1 teaspoon salt

Sauce
1/2 cup mayonnaise
1/4 cup plain yogurt
1 tablespoon fresh lime juice
2 teaspoons grated lime peel
1/4 teaspoon salt

Combine ground beef and seasoning ingredients in large bowl, mixing lightly but thoroughly. Shape into 4 patties, each ¾-inch thick. Place patties on grid over medium, ash-covered coals. Grill, uncovered, 13–15 minutes to medium (160-degree) doneness, until not pink in center and juices show no pink color, turning occasionally. Meanwhile, combine sauce ingredients in small bowl; set aside. Spread sauce on cut sides of rolls. Place a burger on bottom half of each roll; top evenly with watercress or greens. Close sandwiches and serve. Serves 4.

Onion-y Hamburgers

This recipe is not from Texas, but is an easy way to jump-start an otherwise plain burger.

To 2 pounds of ground beef, add 1 pouch of dry onion soup mix and 4 tablespoons of water. Mix well and grill as usual. Serves 4–5.

Chicago Hot Dogs

If you're going to serve hot dogs, you might as well do it right. Here's the Chicago way.

6 beef hot dogs
6 poppy seed hot dog rolls
Yellow mustard
Catsup
Pickle relish (preferably electric green)
1 cup chopped onion
2 tomatoes, cut into small wedges
Pickled peppers — hot ones, for the adults
1 cup drained sauerkraut

Grill the hot dogs as usual, and, if necessary, keep them warm on the grill in a shallow pan of salted water. On a rack, steam the rolls over the hot water for a minute. Set out the condiments and let each kid and adult add their own. If done properly, the hot dogs are completely buried under the condiments and much of the latter falls down your shirt when you bite in. Great with potato salad and baked beans.

Lemon-Grilled Chicken

Lemon, rosemary, and garlic can turn ordinary chicken into a heavenly delight!

3 tablespoons olive oil
3 tablespoons lemon juice
1 tablespoon honey
1 tablespoon fresh rosemary, chopped
Dash salt
3 garlic cloves, minced
3–4 pounds cut-up chicken pieces

Mix together all ingredients (except the chicken) to make a marinade. Put chicken pieces in a large bowl and coat well with the marinade. Cover bowl and chill at least one hour in the fridge. (Overnight will result in more intense flavors.) When ready to grill, place chicken pieces over medium heat. Reserve the extra marinade. Cook for 30 or 40 minutes, turning occasionally and basting with the marinade. Remember that white meat cooks more quickly than dark meat. Serves 6.

Beer Can Chicken

I encountered Beer Can Chicken several years ago, prepared by Pat Kirsop in Stoughton, Wisconsin. It was some of the best, most tender, and most flavorful chicken I have ever had. Later, I found out that the technique goes back at least to the mid-1990s, to the World Championship Barbecue Cooking Contest in Memphis, Tennessee, and maybe before that. Anyway, Beer Can Chicken is no joke. Some people call if Drunken Chicken, others, Chicken on a Throne. Whatever you call it, your guests will call it delicious.

2 cups hickory or oak chips
2 cans of beer
1/2 cup barbecue rub (Pat uses Penzey's Galena
Street Chicken and Rib Rub)
1 6–7 pound roasting chicken (although smaller birds may be used)

On the outdoor grill, use the indirect cooking method. Soak the wood chips in beer for an hour, then drain. Distribute the chips on two sides of the grill, over hot coals, to keep intense heat away from the bird. (If you use a gas grill, put the chips in a smoker box.) Rinse and dry the chicken, then rub the rub liberally over the bird, and force some more under the skin. Spread a couple of teaspoons of rub into the cavity. Open another can of beer, drink a quarter of it, punch two more holes in the lid with a church key, and mix two more teaspoons of rub into the remaining beer. You can also add a few chopped onions, brown sugar, and garlic, if you like. At this point, open another can of beer and this time drink the whole thing. Set the bird onto the first can of beer, lowering the main cavity of the bird over the can. Push the bird's legs slightly forward so that they and the beer can form a tripod to hold the bird upright. Put a drip pan, with a rack, between the coals. Set the chicken gently on the rack, cover the grill, and cook until done. The exact time will depend on the size of the chicken and the intensity of the heat. A temperature reading in the thickest part of the thigh should be at least 165 degrees when the bird is done. The technique works because the flavored steam works upward from the beer can through the chicken, keeping it moist, the excess fat drips easily down into the drip pan, the skin gets nice and crispy, and you don't rip off the back of the chicken upon taking it off the rack. Sheer genius. Before serving, have another can of beer. —*Pat Kirsop*

Barbecued Ribs

If there's some guy in your crowd who takes special pride in his great barbecued ribs, turn him loose! If not, then this good, basic recipe will have to do.

½ cup California brandy
⅓ cup honey
¼ cup vinegar
¼ cup cooking oil
3 tablespoons soy sauce
1 teaspoon Tabasco sauce
2 tablespoons Worcestershire sauce
3 cloves garlic, chopped
4 tablespoons catsup
2 teaspoons Dijon mustard
3 pounds baby back pork ribs, divided into serving sections

(Note: If you're in a hurry, or just lazy, you can buy bottled barbecue sauce and forget about the first 10 ingredients. No shame there.) In a big bowl, combine all the ingredients except the ribs. Then add the ribs and coat them well. Cover, and marinate 4–6 hours, or overnight. Grill over medium, gray coals for 30–40 minutes, turning often and basting with the sauce. Serves 4–6.

Pizza on the Grill
(See page 100)

Corn on the Cob on the Grill

Bringing home a big bag of sweet corn from the roadside stand? You can cook it on the grill without burning it by following these easy directions.

Method No. 1: For each ear, peel back the husk without removing it. Remove the corn silk, then rewrap the husks and tie them with kitchen twine. Soak the corn in water for 1–2 hours before grilling. Shake off excess water. Cook over medium coals for 15–30 minutes, until steam forms, telling you the corn is done.

Method No. 2: Alternatively, you can remove the husks completely, remove the silk, spread with butter, wrap in aluminum foil, pierce with a fork to allow steam to escape, and grill as before.

Method No. 3: What? It's raining? Cook corn in the microwave. Follow method No. 1 through the soaking procedure. Then microwave them on high for 3–5 minutes on a damp paper towel. Turn them over and cook for another 3–5 minutes. Let cool for a minute before removing.

SPECIAL DISHES FOR
Special Kids

HERE ARE A FEW RECIPES especially for the
smaller people in the group. In my hometown we
used to call them children. I don't know what you
call them, but if you serve the following recipes
they'll come when you call them for lunch.

Wiener Winks

The kids will think they're already back in school when you serve this cafeteria fave!

    1 package (16-ounce) hot dogs
    8 single slices American cheese
    8 slices of bread
    8 teaspoons butter

See where we're going with this? Okay, preheat that oven to 350 degrees. Take one slice of bread and spread it with butter. Center one slice of cheese on the buttered bread. Place a hot dog diagonally on the cheese. Gently fold the bread around the hot dog and secure with a toothpick. Do this seven more times with seven more hot dogs. Bake on a cookie sheet or shallow baking pan for 20 to 30 minutes or until golden brown. Serve with potato chips and milk, then sit back and receive the accolades. Makes 8 of the cutest wiener winks you've ever seen.

Corn Dogs

You'll need some wooden skewers for this recipe, but it's lots of fun. Almost like being at the county fair.

    1 cup corn meal
    1 cup all-purpose flour
    2 tablespoons sugar
    2 teaspoons baking powder
    ½ teaspoon salt
    1 egg, slightly beaten
    1 cup milk
    2 tablespoons melted shortening
    1 package (16-ounce) hot dogs
    Oil for deep-fat fryer
    8 wooden skewers, soaked in water

Mix all the dry ingredients. Then add the egg, milk, and melted shortening. Beat well to make a batter. Insert skewers in hot dogs, dip in batter, place dogs skewer-side up in frying basket and fry in deep-fat fryer at 350 degrees until golden brown, about 2 or 3 minutes. Drain on paper towels. Makes 8 dogs.

White Castles

When I was a kid, my dad used to bring home a paper bag full of little White Castle hamburgers—a nickel apiece. (Shows how old I am.) If there isn't a White Castle near your cottage, maybe the kids would like this homemade version.

1 pound ground beef
1 package dry onion soup mix
1 cup grated cheddar cheese
2 tablespoons mayonnaise
Silver dollar hamburger buns
Dill pickle slices

Brown the beef. Add in the soup mix, cheese, and mayonnaise. Spoon some of the mixture on each silver dollar bun (tiny hamburger buns). Add a pickle slice. Wrap in foil and bake at 350 degrees for 15 minutes. Can be made ahead and frozen. Makes 6 little burgers. —*Catherine Tripalin Murray*

Peanut Butter Fudge

Here is an unabashed product-placement recipe, courtesy of the Nestle Corporation. When we steal a recipe, we do it with boldness and élan.

1½ cups sugar
⅔ cup (5-ounce can) CARNATION Evaporated Milk
2 tablespoons butter or margarine
¼ teaspoon salt
2 cups miniature marshmallows
1½ cups (9 ounces) NESTLE TOLL HOUSE Semi-Sweet Chocolate Morsels
1 cup chunky or regular peanut butter
1 teaspoon vanilla extract
½ cup chopped peanuts (optional)

Combine sugar, evaporated milk, butter, and salt in a medium, heavy-duty saucepan. Bring to a full rolling boil over medium heat, stirring constantly. Boil, stirring constantly, 4 to 5 minutes. Remove from heat.

Stir in marshmallows, morsels, peanut butter, and vanilla extract. Stir vigorously for a minute or until marshmallows are melted. Pour into foil-lined 8-inch square baking pan. Cool for 1 minute. Top with peanuts, pressing in slightly. Chill for 2 hours or until firm. Lift from pan, remove foil, and cut into pieces.

Corn Flake Cookies

> 1 cup sugar
> 1 cup white corn syrup
> 1½ cups peanut butter (smooth or chunky)
> 4 cups corn flakes cereal

Line a shallow baking pan or cookie sheet with waxed paper. In a cooking pot, combine the sugar and corn syrup and heat until it comes to a boil, stirring gently. Add the peanut butter and continue stirring until the mixture is smooth. Stir in the corn flakes and turn off heat. Drop teaspoonfuls of the mixture onto the baking pan. When slightly cooled, press the cookies flatter with a fork. If you have M&Ms, you can press them into the cookies. Makes about 16 cookies.

S'Mores

It's a darn shame that summer camps don't teach kids how to make S'mores any more. Now they teach them how to develop computer software, trade options in the stock market, and fight global warming. Well, here's a recipe every kid should know, whether at camp or cottage. Keep the tradition alive!

> 1 Hershey's chocolate bar
> 2 or 3 big marshmallows
> 2 graham crackers

Toast the marshmallows over coals or campfire. Break the chocolate bar in half. Place one half on top of one graham cracker. Put the marshmallows on top of this. Then the other half of the chocolate bar, then the other graham cracker, to make a sandwich. Eat. Repeat several times. Jump in the lake to wash yourself off.

Fish Tank

Here's a fun recipe for kids, from the Blue Plate Diner Cookbook. You'll need some clear drinking glasses for this one.

  3-ounce package "Berry Blue" Jell-O
  2 dozen gummy fish

Follow the package directions to make the Jell-O. Pour into the glasses and cool. Just as the Jell-O begins to set, add the gummy fish to each glass and stir them into the Jell-O. Continue to cool the Jell-O until it is firm. Let the kids marvel at the fish in the "tank." (Did you know that Jell-O is more than a hundred years old? We ALL grew up on Jell-O. Ditto for Cracker Jack and Shredded Wheat.) Makes 4 to 8 tanks, depending on the size of the glasses.

Smoothies

If you have a blender at the cottage, the kids can make up their own smoothies with the fresh fruits you just picked up at the roadside stand, combined with ice cream, or yogurt, or orange juice, or milk. The amazing thing is, smoothies can not only be delicious, they can also be good for kids! What a concept! Here are just a few recipes. You'll have many more of your own.

Peachy Cream Smoothie

  1 cup milk
  1 tablespoon sugar
  1 cup vanilla yogurt
  2 fresh peaches, peeled and sliced

Blend for one minute.

Chocolate Banana Smoothie

½ cup milk
½ cup orange juice
2 tablespoons chocolate syrup
1 banana

Blend for one minute.

Banana Peanut Smoothie

1 cup milk
1 cup vanilla yogurt
1 large banana
¼ cup roasted peanuts

Blend for one minute.

Strawberry Banana Smoothie

1 cup milk
1 cup vanilla yogurt
4 large strawberries (or 1 cup frozen strawberries)
1 small banana, cut up

Blend for one minute.

Caramel Corn

How to turn ordinary popcorn into something really special—something that will really gum up the kids' braces—but is oh so good.

⅓ cup butter or margarine
⅔ cup packed brown sugar
⅓ cup light corn syrup
¼ teaspoon baking soda
½ teaspoon vanilla
10 cups popped popcorn

Cook butter in a saucepan until melted. Stir in the brown sugar and corn syrup. Continue cooking until the mixture comes to a boil, stirring several times. Let boil for 3 minutes without stirring, then stir in soda and vanilla. Add all the popcorn and blend in well with the gooey stuff. Cook on medium heat for 1 minute, then stir. Cook on medium heat for another minute, then stir again to coat popcorn well. Spread out mixture on a cookie sheet and let cool completely. Break apart and store in tightly sealed container. Makes a bunch.

(Also see the section on desserts, which has many recipes that kids can help make.)

VEGETABLES, SALADS,
& Side Dishes

Not Really Homemade Baked Beans

They'll swear you spent all day cooking these beans. Only you and I will know the truth. (I've tried all the baked beans, and B&M are the best for this recipe. The B&M company did not pay me to say this, but if they want to send a couple cases, I wouldn't complain.)

> 55-ounce can B&M Original Baked Beans
> Small can butter beans
> 3 slabs bacon
> 1 small onion, chopped
> Catsup or chili sauce
> Dijon mustard
> Molasses (light or dark)
> Tabasco sauce
> Worcestershire sauce

The proportions of seasonings are strictly to taste. So begin with a little of everything, then add more as you taste and continue cooking. Some like sweeter beans, some spicier. Empty the baked beans in a large saucepan. Drain the butter beans and add them, too. Fry the bacon just short of crisp and cut it into little pieces. Sauté the onions in the bacon fat until soft. Add bacon and onions to beans. Then add about a ¼ cup of catsup, the same amount of mustard, and of molasses, and a couple dashes of Tabasco and Worcestershire. Stir gently until well blended. Let simmer on very low heat for 30 minutes, then taste and adjust seasonings. Do not overcook, or the beans will turn to mush and the secret will be out. Serves 6 as a side dish.

Baked Lima Beans

This recipe is more work than you might want to spend, but the results are terrific. Soak the beans overnight and make up the recipe the next day.

> 1 pound large dry lima beans
> ¾ pound bacon
> 1 large onion, coarsely chopped
> ½ teaspoon salt
> 1 tablespoon cornstarch
> 1 teaspoon dry mustard
> 3½ tablespoons dark molasses

¼ teaspoon black pepper
⅛ cup brown sugar +
½ cup brown sugar

(1) After soaking beans overnight, rinse them well, cover with water, bring to a boil, then turn off heat and let soak for 1 hour. Drain the beans and dump them in a soup pot with the bacon lying on top. Add salt and just cover with water. Cook over low heat until beans are barely tender, about 45 minutes. Don't let them get mushy. (2) Remove the bacon and set aside. Drain and save the liquid from the beans. Place beans in a casserole dish about 1½ inches deep. Lay strips of bacon on top. (3) Mix the cornstarch and mustard with small amount of cold bean liquid and set aside. Bring rest of bean liquid to boil, add the molasses, pepper, and ⅛ cup of brown sugar. Add the cornstarch mixture to the simmering liquid and stir until blended. Slowly pour the liquid over beans in the casserole, almost to the level of the bacon. Sprinkle ½ cup of brown sugar on top. Bake at 350 degrees for 2 hours, then reduce heat to 250 and bake 30 minutes more. If beans seem dry, sprinkle a little water on top. Serves 6–8 as a side dish.

Glazed Carrots

Some kids who don't like carrots like these carrots, because they don't taste like carrots, they taste like candy. Okay, so they taste like candy carrots.

Pare one-half pound of whole carrots and boil in a saucepan until almost tender. Drain and pat dry. Roll in sugar. Return to saucepan and simmer in one-half stick of melted butter, turning often, until glazed.

Optional, for oven-browned carrots: Preheat oven to 375. In 1½-quart casserole, lay down a pound of pared carrots, cut into 2-inch pieces. Add ¼ cup hot water, 2 tablespoons butter, ¼ cup brown sugar, and 1½ teaspoons salt. Bake covered for 30 minutes. Remove cover and bake another 15 minutes or until tender.

Grits Soufflé

Here is a good recipe from Susan Jenkins, originally from Mississippi, now of Virginia, who insists, "You don't have to be southern to love grits." We'll see.

1½ cups regular grits
5 cups boiling water
2 teaspoons seasoned salt
1 teaspoon onion salt
1 teaspoon garlic salt
¾ teaspoon Worcestershire sauce
½ cup butter or margarine
3 eggs
½ to 1 pound longhorn or mild cheddar cheese, cubed
Paprika

Cook grits in boiling water for 5 minutes. Stir in salts, Worcestershire sauce, and butter. Stir 2 to 3 tablespoons of grits into beaten eggs, then stir egg mixture into the remainder of the grits. Add cheese and stir until the cheese is melted. Pour into a buttered 2-quart soufflé dish and sprinkle with paprika. Cover and refrigerate overnight (also can cook right away). Uncover and bake at 350 degrees for 90 minutes. Enjoy! —*Susan Jenkins*

Gallo Pinto

Gallo pinto ("GUY-oh PEEN-toe") is a Costa Rican national specialty, but variations are found throughout the tropical world. It's cheap to make, and the combination of beans and rice form a complete protein for vegetarians. Here is one good recipe.

2 cups dry kidney beans, soaked and drained
4 tablespoons olive oil
1 medium onion, finely chopped
1 garlic clove, minced
2 medium tomatoes, peeled, seeded, and chopped
1 bay leaf
Salt and pepper to taste
3½ cups chicken broth
1 cup long-grain white rice

Soak the kidney beans overnight. In a skillet, sauté the onion and garlic in hot olive oil until the onion is soft but not brown. Add the tomatoes, bay leaf, salt, and pepper. Bring to a simmer, then add the beans and stock and bring to a boil. Reduce the heat and simmer for 90 minutes until beans are almost tender. Watch the pot and add more broth if necessary. Add the rice, cover, and simmer for 25 minutes more. (For

vegetarians, you may substitute water for chicken broth.) Serves 6–8 as
a side dish.

Monday Red Beans and Rice

Down in Cajun Country, Monday means red beans and rice. But even up
in the North Woods, you can "eat mo bettah" with this good recipe. Just
remember to set the beans to soaking before you go to bed Sunday night.

    1 pound dried red beans, cleaned and sorted
    8 cups cold water
    1/2 pound bacon, ham, or salt pork, diced
    1 tablespoon olive oil
    1 cup finely chopped onion
    2 cloves garlic, minced
    2 tablespoons chopped parsley
    3/4 teaspoon salt
    1 1/2 teaspoons Tabasco sauce
    4 cups hot cooked rice

Soak the beans overnight in water. The next day, add the meat, bring to
a boil, reduce the heat and simmer for 15 minutes. While this is cooking, sauté the onion and garlic in hot oil for several minutes, until tender but not brown. Add this to the beans along with the parsley, salt,
and Tabasco sauce. Cover and simmer for 90–120 minutes, stirring occasionally, until the beans are tender. (You may have to add a little water
if the beans get uncovered.) Serve over hot cooked rice. Serves 6–8.

Buck Camp Taters

2 tablespoons virgin olive oil
1 large yellow onion, chopped
4 cloves garlic, minced
8 medium potatoes, peeled and diced
½ pound bulk of your favorite sausage, crumbled
2 medium yams, peeled and diced
1 green pepper
3 bay leaves
1 tablespoon herb and garlic mix (Emeril's Essence is perfect)
½ tablespoon ground pepper
½ tablespoon coarse kosher salt or sea salt

Heat olive oil in large nonstick pan or electric skillet. Cook onion until soft, about 5 minutes. Add the garlic and cook for 2 more minutes. Add all other ingredients to the pan. Cook uncovered, stirring to brown potatoes evenly, for about 10 minutes. Add ¼–½ cup water. Cover, but not completely, to allow steam to escape, and cook until the potatoes and yams are tender, about 20 minutes. Serves 10–12.

If this is truly at "Buck Camp" and someone in the group has actually bagged a deer, slicing and dicing a fresh venison tenderloin into the mix makes for a wonderful one-pan meal. Eat it before the warden knocks on the door! —*from an unnamed buck camper*

Sauerkraut

How to take a can of ordinary sauerkraut and make it into great sauerkraut.

15-ounce can sauerkraut
¼ teaspoon caraway seeds
¼ teaspoon salt
1 teaspoon prepared mustard
⅛ teaspoon white pepper
1 tablespoon onions, minced
½ cup bacon fat

Mix everything together and cook in skillet over medium heat until it turns golden yellow. Great with baked beans and grilled brats. Serves 4 as a side dish.

Red Cabbage with Apple

Here's a good German dish to serve with pork, ham, or wild game.

1 large red cabbage
3 tablespoons butter
3 apples, peeled, cored, and sliced as for pie
2 tablespoons molasses
1 onion, chopped very fine
Juice of 1 lemon
1/2 cup dry red wine
Salt to taste

Remove the outer leaves from the cabbage and shred the rest of it. In a large pot or Dutch oven, melt the butter and throw in the cabbage, apples, and molasses. Cook over medium heat for several minutes, until all ingredients are well blended. Add the onion, lemon, wine, and salt, cover pot, and simmer for an hour or more. Check occasionally to see that it doesn't dry out. If it begins to dry, add a little apple juice or cider. Serves 4–6 as a side dish.

Tartar Sauce

A great accompaniment to all those fish you pull out of the lake.

1/2 cup mayonnaise
1 tablespoon minced onion
2 tablespoons minced celery leaves and stems
1/4 cup dill pickle relish

Mix all ingredients well, and refrigerate before serving.

Johnny Cakes

You can make these easily while you are frying up some other foods. Call it multitasking.

1 egg, beaten
2 cups corn meal
1 teaspoon salt
1 1/4 cups milk

Mix all ingredients to form a batter. Drop spoonfuls of batter onto a well-greased hot griddle or drop into deep fat fryer. Cook to golden brown and serve hot with syrup and butter. Makes 12 cakes.

Superb Potato Salad

Best recipe: Go to the grocery store and buy some deli potato salad in a plastic tub. But if you must show off, here is a superb recipe made with fancy French dressing.

For dressing
1/4 teaspoon salt
1/4 teaspoon pepper
6 tablespoons olive oil
2 tablespoons lemon juice
1/4 teaspoon dry mustard
1 clove garlic, minced

Other essential ingredients
2 pounds red potatoes
6 eggs
1 large onion

Optional ingredients
Salad olives
Pickles or pickle relish
Celery
Cucumber
Fresh dill

To make dressing: (1) combine in small bowl salt, pepper, 1 tablespoon olive oil, 1 tablespoon lemon juice, and the dry mustard. Beat until smooth. (2) Add 2 tablespoons olive oil and beat well again. (3) Add 1 tablespoon lemon juice, 3 tablespoons olive oil, and the garlic. Shake well and refrigerate. (4) Boil the potatoes in their jackets. Hard-boil the eggs. (5) Peel the potatoes and marinate them in the dressing while still warm. Chop the onion and all but one of the eggs and add to the potatoes. You may also add some chopped salad olives, pickles, celery, cucumber, or some fresh dill leaves—as you wish. If you want a creamier consistency, add some mayonnaise. Refrigerate for at least one hour. Top with the last egg, sliced, and a sprinkling of paprika. Now, don't you wish you had just gone down to the grocery store and bought some in a plastic tub? Serves 8 as a side dish.

Pesto Pasta Salad

This one is for when you get tired of potato salad.

1 pound rotini spirals, cooked and drained
1 medium red or green pepper, diced
1 large, ripe tomato, chopped
½ cup pesto
3 tablespoons vinegar
½ teaspoon salt
Dash of black pepper
2 cloves minced garlic
¼ cup grated Parmesan cheese
1 small onion, chopped

Combine all ingredients and chill at least 2 hours. Serves 8 as a side dish.

Tuna-Artichoke Salad

The beauty of this recipe is its versatility. It calls for artichoke hearts, fresh tomatoes, onions, and olives, but you can just as easily add or substitute garbanzo beans, green beans, sweet green pepper, cucumber, or pimientos. Use your imagination and use up some vegetables you have on hand, for a great summertime salad.

    12-ounce box of bow tie pasta
    Small jar marinated artichoke hearts, quartered
    2 medium tomatoes, diced
    1½ cups diced mozzarella or other soft cheese
    Small can black olives, drained
    ½ cup sliced sweet red onions
    ½ cup fresh basil leaves, cut up
    12-ounce bottle creamy Italian salad dressing
    6-ounce can good-quality tuna, in oil
    Salt and pepper to taste

Cook the pasta according to directions (do not overcook), drain, and cool. Mix pasta with all other ingredients, gently breaking apart the tuna. Cover and chill for at least 1 hour, or overnight. Serves 8.

Chicken Salad

Here is a basic recipe that you can make from that leftover chicken.

    2 cups chopped cooked chicken breast
    ½ cup chopped celery
    2 tablespoons finely chopped onion
    4 tablespoons mayonnaise
    4 tablespoons plain yogurt
    ¼ teaspoon pepper

Mix all ingredients together. Serve in sandwiches, or hollow out large tomatoes and fill with chicken salad for Tomato Surprise! (For an extra fruity kick, add a little crushed pineapple.) Serves 4–6.

Wisconsin Apple and Chicken Salad

Add a fruity touch to your chicken salad with Wisconsin apples! You could also try it with tart cherries.

2 cups shredded cabbage
1 cup tart Wisconsin apples—McIntosh or Jonathan
½ cup coarsely chopped walnuts or pecans
½ cup chopped celery
¾ cup mayonnaise
1 cup cooked chicken, cubed

Mix together all ingredients and chill several hours or overnight. Serves 4.

Wisconsin Apple Salad

1 cup cottage cheese
½ cup mayonnaise
½ teaspoon nutmeg
2 cups chopped Wisconsin apples
2 tablespoons raisins
1 banana, sliced or ½ cup seedless grapes

In a blender, blend the cottage cheese, mayonnaise, and nutmeg until smooth. Pour into a bowl and fold in the apples, raisins, and banana. Serves 6-8.

Vinegar-y Coleslaw

This coleslaw is tart enough to form a pleasant balance to the grease from the chicken or meat course.

1 large head cabbage, shredded
1 large onion, finely chopped
2 green peppers, chopped
1 cup celery, chopped
1¾ cups sugar
1 teaspoon mustard seed
2 teaspoons salt, or to taste
⅔ cup cider vinegar

In a large bowl, mix together the cabbage, onion, pepper, and celery. Then blend in the other ingredients. Cover and chill for several hours or overnight. Serves 8.

Deli Coleslaw Made Better

Everyone will think that you made this coleslaw yourself. Well, you did, sort of.

 2 pounds prepared store-bought coleslaw mix
 ½ onion, diced
 2 stalks celery, diced
 ½ green pepper, diced

 Dressing
 ½ cup olive oil
 Juice from ½ lime
 Salt, pepper, and garlic powder to taste
 1 tablespoon sugar
 Vinegar to taste

Mix slaw, onion, celery, and pepper into bowl and toss. Mix dressing ingredients in a jar and shake well. Pour dressing over coleslaw mixture. Toss slaw with dressing three times, 5 minutes apart. Chill well and serve. Serves 8 as a side dish. —*James Novak*

Watercress Salad

Lucky you—you found a secret stream with a big crop of watercress!

 ¼ cup mayonnaise
 1 or 2 teaspoons honey
 3 cups fresh watercress (or may be mixed with some baby spinach)
 1 medium carrot, grated
 2 eggs, hard-boiled and diced

Chill all ingredients. Blend mayonnaise and honey to make dressing. Toss dressing with other ingredients and serve immediately. Serves 6.

Three-Bean Salad

This recipe is so traditional American Midwest, you'll think you're at a Lutheran church social.

1 can yellow string beans
1 can green string beans
1 can kidney beans
½ cup olive oil
½ cup vinegar
½ cup sugar
Garlic salt or powder to taste
½ teaspoon dry mustard
Parsley flakes

Drain beans and cut string beans to bite size. Mix dressing and combine all. Chill before serving. Serves 8 as a side dish. — *Connie Thompson*

American Tuna Salad

This is a little more elegant than most tuna salads, but also a little better.

¾ cup mayonnaise
½ cup sour cream
¼ cup cucumber, peeled and diced
½ teaspoon dillweed
2 tablespoons onion, finely chopped
2 hard-boiled eggs
1½ cups lettuce or spring greens
2 cans tuna (6½-ounce each)
Fresh tomato wedges

Blend together mayonnaise, sour cream, cucumbers, dillweed, and onions. Chop the egg whites (not the yolks) and add them into the mixture. Chill. (No, not you — chill the *mixture*.) Flake the tuna. For each plate, top the lettuce with tuna and dressing. Crumble the egg yolks on top, and serve with tomato wedges. Serves 6–8 elegantly.

Indian Wild Rice Corn Pudding

This takes a little longer than we like to spend in the cottage kitchen, but it's worth it.

⅓ cup uncooked wild rice
1½ cups whole kernel corn, drained
3 eggs, well beaten
1 small onion, minced
¼ cup all-purpose flour
1½ teaspoon salt
Dash pepper
Dash nutmeg
1 teaspoon sugar
1 tablespoons melted butter
2 cups light cream
1 jar pimientos, drained and chopped

Cook wild rice according to package directions. Combine the cooked wild rice, corn, eggs, and onions. Combine flour, salt, pepper, sugar, and nutmeg and stir into corn mixture. Add butter, cream, and pimientos and mix all well. Pour into buttered 2-quart shallow baking dish. Set dish in larger pan and pour hot water to 1-inch depth around inner dish. Bake at 325 degrees uncovered for 1 hour or until pudding is firm and knife inserted in center comes out clean. Cut into squares and serve hot. Serves 4–6.

Wild Rice Hot Dish

Here is a recipe passed along to me by Olga Schmidt, or "Granny," as we used to know her at the old Trophy Tap in Madison, Wisconsin. It's a good one (as was Granny).

1 cup wild rice
½ pound bacon, cut into small pieces
1 cup chopped celery
1 medium onion, chopped
1 can condensed cream of mushroom soup
1 can button mushrooms, drained

Place wild rice in 2 quarts of boiling water, boil for 30 minutes and drain. Fry bacon until just crisp. Drain off grease, but reserve just enough to sauté the celery and onions. Combine all ingredients with one cup of water in a casserole dish. Cover and bake at 350 degrees for 1 hour. Add water if necessary as it cooks. Serves 4 as a side dish.

Just Plain Rice

Do you have trouble making rice? Here is my never-fail recipe, given to me many years ago by my friend Sam Diman. Believe me, it never fails.

Mix 1 part rice with 2 parts water. Add salt. Bring to full boil. Then cover and turn down heat low. Simmer 25 minutes and DO NOT UN-COVER AT ANY TIME. Voila—perfect rice. (For more flavor, you can substitute chicken broth for water.)

Ham Salad

One more way to make that leftover ham stretch just a little further.

1½ cups finely chopped or minced cooked ham
1 cup sliced celery
4 scallions, sliced
1 teaspoon lemon juice or cider vinegar
⅛ teaspoon black or white pepper
2 hard-boiled eggs, chopped
⅓ cup mayonnaise or salad dressing
2 tablespoons sweet pickle relish
2 teaspoons prepared mustard
Paprika

Mix together ham, celery, scallions, lemon juice, and pepper. Blend in eggs, mayonnaise, pickle relish, and mustard. Cover and chill at least 1 hour. Sprinkle with paprika before serving. Makes sandwiches for 6. (Hint: For Tomato Surprise! hollow out a large, fresh tomato and stuff it with the ham salad. Serve on a lettuce leaf.)

Deviled Eggs

Come on, what's a picnic without deviled eggs?

12 large eggs
5 tablespoons mayonnaise
2 tablespoons sweet pickle relish
½ teaspoon Tabasco sauce
½ teaspoon prepared mustard
Dash soy sauce
Salt and pepper to taste
Paprika

Hard-boil the eggs and cool. Peel and slice each egg in half, lengthwise. Remove the yolks, put them in a small bowl, and mash them with a fork. Add all the other ingredients except the paprika, and mash it all together until nice and creamy. Spoon the yolk mixture back into the egg white halves, peak it up real pretty, and sprinkle with just a little paprika. There—just like grandma used to make. Makes (let's see, 12 X 2) oh yeah, 24 deviled egg halves.

Gazpacho

Here is a refreshing cold salad that uses all the wonderful summer vegetables you pick up at the roadside stand. Sealed in a jar, it will keep for a week in the fridge.

3 cucumbers, peeled
6 medium tomatoes, seeded
1 medium onion
2 green peppers, seeded
1 envelope dry Italian salad dressing mix
Red wine vinegar

Chop all vegetables fine, then drain. Place all in a 2-quart jar. Prepare the dressing according to package directions, using red wine vinegar. Pour the dressing over vegetables in jar, making sure there are no air spaces left. Shake to distribute dressing among vegetables and refrigerate at least 4 hours before serving. Serves 6–8 as a side dish.

Hula Spam Pizza

I don't know why I'm including this recipe in this book. Maybe because it's one of the worst-sounding recipes I've ever come across. Then, again, that little Spam part of me, way over in a back corner of my stomach, says, why not try it? (But then, it said the same thing about the Mock Apple Pie recipe that appeared on the Ritz Cracker box in the 1960s. For those of you too young to remember, there were no apples used.)

    12-inch prepared pizza crust
    6 ounces sliced provolone
    12-ounce can Spam, cut into thin squares, or into portraits of your favorite sports heroes
    ½ cup thinly sliced sweet red onion
    ½ cup chopped sweet green pepper
    1 can chunk pineapple, drained

Preheat the oven to 425 degrees. Grease a pizza pan and press the crust into the pan. Lay in the cheese first, then all the other ingredients. Bake 25–30 minutes, until crust is golden brown and crispy and the Spam is bubbly and indescribably tempting. Call in the kids, then go out for dinner.

Soups

Watercress Soup

Lucky you, if you can find a crop of watercress growing nearby in a cold, quick-running stream.

    3 good-size bunches fresh watercress
    2 tablespoons butter
    2 tablespoons all-purpose flour
    6 cups boiling water
    Salt and pepper to taste
    3 tablespoons white rice
    1 egg yolk

Wash and chop watercress finely. Saute in butter for 8 minutes. Sprinkle with flour and slowly add the boiling water while stirring. Simmer 15 minutes. Add salt, pepper, and rice. Cook at a slow boil for 18–20 minutes. Blend the egg yolk well into the soup just before serving. Serves 4–6.

Cold Cuke Soup

This is from one of my vegetarian friends. It's a great cold soup for a hot day. It will keep for a day or two in the refrigerator, but not much longer.

    2 large cucumbers, shredded
    1 garlic clove, crushed
    2–3 tablespoons oil
    ¾ cup walnuts, chopped
    3 cups plain yogurt
    ½ cup sour cream
    Fresh salt and pepper to taste
    2 tablespoons chopped fresh dill

Shred cukes. (Be careful not to shred your knuckles. This is supposed to be a vegetarian soup.) Sprinkle with salt and refrigerate for half an hour while you do the next step, which is: Combine garlic, oil, walnuts, and yogurt in a blender. Add sour cream and blend. Add pepper. Then combine yogurt mixture with cukes, sprinkle with fresh dill (or tarragon if you prefer) and some chopped walnuts. Serves 6–8. — *Caroline Beckett*

Minestrone

No dish is more forgiving than minestrone—you can make it out of almost any vegetables and starch on hand. To make it really Italian, though, you must start with a good Italian sausage and basil. Here's one good recipe that you can play around with at will.

    ½ pound bulk Italian sausage
    1 tablespoon olive oil
    1 cup onions, chopped
    2 garlic cloves, minced
    1 teaspoon dried basil
    2 small zucchinis, sliced
    16-ounce can diced tomatoes, undrained
    2 cans beef broth (10 ounces each)
    Salt and pepper to taste
    16-ounce can white kidney beans, great northern
    beans, or garbanzos
    ½ cup dry pasta (small shape such as shells, macaroni, or rigatoni)
    ½ cup dry red wine
    Grated Parmesan or Romano cheese

In soup kettle, brown the sausage in olive oil. Add the onion, garlic, and basil and cook for 5 minutes. Add the zucchini, tomatoes, beef broth, salt, and pepper. Simmer for one hour. Add the beans, pasta, and wine and cook until pasta is tender but not mushy. Pass around the grated cheese at the table. Serve with hearty European-style bread and a simple salad for a great meal anytime. Serves 4–6.

Ham and Bean Soup

Here's another good way to use up that extra ham.

    3–4 cups water
    1 large ham bone and/or ham scraps
    1½ cups chopped celery
    1 cup chopped onion
    ¾ teaspoon dried thyme
    1 teaspoon ham base (or ½ teaspoon salt)
    ¼ teaspoon black pepper
    1 bay leaf (optional)
    15-ounce can navy beans (or other white beans)

In kettle, combine water with all other ingredients except beans. Simmer, covered, 45–50 minutes. Remove kettle from heat. Remove ham bone, cool it, and pick off good meat, returning it to the kettle. Add beans, undrained. This soup can wait in the refrigerator until dinnertime. Then, just heat through and serve with good bread or cornbread. (Of course, you can also make this with dried beans, rehydrated overnight.) Serves 4.

Stuffed Green Pepper Soup

Here is a good and easy-to-prepare soup for a cool, rainy day. And it's even better reheated the next day. (As my Pennsylvania Dutch great-grandmother used to say, "It's better after it sleeps!")

1½ pounds ground beef
1 medium to large onion, chopped
6 cups beef broth (49-ounce can)
18-ounce can crushed tomatoes
1 can condensed tomato soup (10.75-ounce can)
1 cup catsup
4 large green peppers, coarsely chopped
Salt and pepper to taste
2 cups cooked rice

Brown the ground beef and onion. Add beef broth and bring to a boil. Add crushed tomatoes, tomato soup, catsup, and green peppers. Add salt and pepper. Cover and simmer 2 hours, stirring occasionally. Add cooked rice, heat through, and serve. Serves 6. —*Catherine Tripalin Murray*

Leftover Mashed Potato Soup

Don't tell anybody this was made from leftovers. They'll never know, and it will be our little secret. Besides, it's their fault if they didn't eat all the mashed potatoes last night.

2 cups leftover mashed potatoes
4 tablespoons butter
1 cup chopped onion
1 quart whole milk
Chopped parsley or chives
Salt and pepper to taste

Lemon Meringue
2 egg whites
4 tablespoons sugar
1 teaspoon lemon juice

Mix the sugar, flour, salt, and cornstarch. Add the egg yolks and milk.
Cook over low heat until very thick and smooth, stirring constantly.
Cool. Cover bottom of a baked pie shell (or graham cracker shell) with
sliced bananas. Pour in cream filling and cover. Make Lemon Meringue:
Beat egg whites stiff. Blend in sugar and lemon juice. Top pie with
meringue and bake in slow oven (275 degrees) until meringue peaks are
golden brown.

Banana Nut Bread

Still got unused bananas? Here's the traditional way to get rid of them.
And banana bread is great when used to make French toast in the morning. Just dip slices in beaten egg, fry 'em up, and serve with real maple
syrup.

1/3 cup shortening
1/2 cup sugar
2 eggs
1 3/4 cup flour
1 teaspoon baking powder
1/2 teaspoon baking soda
1/2 teaspoon salt
1 cup bananas, mashed
Chopped walnuts or pecans (optional)

Cream shortening and sugar. Add eggs and beat well. Add dry ingredients and bananas and mix well. Pour into well-greased 9x5x3-inch pan.
Bake at 350 degrees for 45–50 minutes. Makes one loaf for 6.

Sour Cream Raspberry Pie

This was a smash hit at my last picnic. And that wasn't even in the North Woods!

3½ cups sour cream
4 egg yolks
2 cups sugar
⅓ cup flour
⅔ cup dry (not prepared) raspberry gelatin
5–6 cups fresh raspberries
11-inch prebaked piecrust, in foil piepan
Whipped cream or whipped topping

In a large pan, cream together the sour cream and egg yolks. Add sugar and flour and stir until smooth. Cook over medium heat, stirring constantly, until pudding is thick and pulls away from the pan when flipped toward you. Do not undercook or pie will be runny. Remove from heat. Blend in raspberry gelatin. Let cool 10–15 minutes. Blend in fresh raspberries very gently, so they don't break apart. Pour into pastry crust. Refrigerate. When thoroughly chilled, top with whipped cream and serve. Serves 8–10.

Maple Syrup Pie with Meringue

1 cup maple syrup
½ cup whole milk
½ cup light cream
1 tablespoon unsalted butter
1 tablespoon vanilla extract
3 egg yolks, beaten (save the whites!)
1 baked pie shell (9-inch)
3 egg whites
½ cup granulated sugar

Bring maple syrup to a boil in a saucepan. Add milk and cream, stir, and cook over low heat — but do not boil. Add butter, vanilla extract, and egg yolks. Stir and cook over low heat until mixture thickens. Pour mixture into baked pie shell and set aside. Preheat oven to 180 degrees. To make meringue, place egg whites and sugar in double boiler. Mix with an electric beater at low heat until mixture thickens and forms peaks. Spread mixture over pie and cook in 180-degree oven until meringue peaks are golden brown, about 10 minutes. Serves 8.

Quick Cheesecake

16 ounces softened cream cheese
½ cup sugar
½ teaspoon vanilla extract
2 eggs
9-inch prepared graham cracker crust

Beat together cream cheese, sugar, and vanilla extract until smooth. Add eggs and blend again until smooth. Pour into prepared crust and bake at 350 degrees for 50 minutes or until center is almost set. Cool. Refrigerate 3 hours or overnight before serving. Top with fresh berries, if you got 'em.

Cinnamon-Sour Cream Coffee Cake

This is an easy recipe for a cinnamon coffee cake, one that will fill the cottage with a delightful aroma as your guests are staggering out of their bedrooms. The recipe calls for a Bundt pan, but you can improvise with another baking pan.

1 cup butter
2 cups granulated sugar
2 large eggs
2 cups flour
1 teaspoon baking powder
¼ teaspoon salt
1 teaspoon vanilla extract
1 cup sour cream
2½ tablespoons brown sugar
¾ teaspoon cinnamon

Cream together the butter and sugar until the butter is soft and fluffy. Blend in the eggs and mix well. Add in the flour, baking powder, and salt, then the vanilla extract. Fold in the sour cream to make batter. Pour one-half of the batter into the bottom of a Bundt pan or 9x9-inch baking pan.

Mix together the brown sugar and cinnamon and sprinkle this over the batter. Then top with the remaining batter. Bake at 325 degrees for one hour or until top is brown and a knife comes out clean. Serves 6.

Strawberries and Sour Cream Custard

Strawberries never tasted so good!

 ½ cup sugar
 2½ tablespoons cornstarch
 ¼ teaspoon salt
 1½ cups milk
 4 eggs, beaten
 ½ cup sour cream
 1½ teaspoons vanilla
 1 to 2 pints fresh strawberries, halved or sliced

In a saucepan, combine the sugar, cornstarch, and salt. Gradually stir in the milk. Cook over medium heat, stirring constantly, until mixture boils. Boil and stir for 1 minute more. Remove from heat. Blend the beaten eggs into the milk mixture. Then add the sour cream and vanilla and beat with a wire whisk until well blended. Cool immediately by placing in a bowl of ice or cold water for 10 minutes. Cover and refrigerate. To serve, spoon the custard over strawberries.

Cranberry Bread

 2 cups flour
 ½ cup packed brown sugar
 2 teaspoons baking powder
 ¼ teaspoon salt
 ¾ cup cran-apple juice
 ¼ cup vegetable oil
 1 egg
 1 teaspoon vanilla
 1 cup fresh cranberries, chopped
 ½ cup walnuts (optional)

Preheat oven to 350 degrees. Grease a loaf pan. Mix all ingredients thoroughly, except cranberries and walnuts. Then carefully blend in cranberries and walnuts. Transfer to loaf pan and bake 55–60 minutes at 350 degrees. Serves 6.

Fresh Fruit Cobbler

4 tablespoons butter, creamed
1/2 cup sugar
1 cup flour
2 teaspoons baking powder
1/2 cup milk
2–3 cups of berries in season
1 cup sugar

Mix the creamed butter, 1/2 cup sugar, flour, baking powder, and milk. Put all in a buttered dish. Cover with a few cups of berries. Sift 1 cup sugar on top (less, if you don't like it so sweet). Add a scant 1/2 cup hot water. Bake 1 hour in a moderate oven (350 degrees). Serve with whipped cream if desired. Serves 6.

Easier Fruit Cobbler

Everyone will think you made this from scratch with fresh fruit. (All right, they won't, but they'll eat it anyway.)

21-ounce can fruit pie filling
1 1/4 cups Bisquick
1 tablespoon granulated sugar
1/4 cup milk
1/4 cup sour cream

To sprinkle on top
1 more tablespoon granulated sugar
1/2 teaspoon cinnamon

Preheat oven to 425 degrees. In a pot, heat the fruit filling to boiling. Pour into a greased 1 1/2-quart casserole. Mix together the Bisquick, 1 tablespoon sugar, milk, and sour cream into a dough. Drop dollops of dough onto hot fruit filling in casserole. Sprinkle with a mixture of 1 tablespoon sugar and ½ teaspoon cinnamon. Bake till biscuits are golden brown, about 20 minutes. Serves 4–6.

Peach Whip

Mash enough skinned ripe peaches to make one cup of puree. Beat 2 egg whites until they are stiff, add 2 tablespoons sugar, and continue to beat the whites until they are stiff and a little shiny. Add 2 more tablespoons sugar and the peach puree and beat the mixture thoroughly. Spoon the mixture into glasses and chill it. Serve very cold, topped with whipped cream.

Cherries Jubilee

Here is a recipe for the final night at the cottage. A flaming delight!

    1 can (16 ounces) black pitted cherries
    2 cups sugar
    1 cup cornstarch
    2 slices lemon
    ½ cup port wine
    ½ cup brandy
    2 pints vanilla ice cream or 6 pieces plain cake

Into a chafing dish or small saucepan, pour juice from cherries, and boil until reduced to ½ cup. Mix sugar and cornstarch well, and stir into juice. Heat and stir until clear. Add cherries, lemon slices, and port. Reheat. Meanwhile, have your assistant dish up the ice cream or cake. Heat brandy slightly, pour over cherries, and touch with a lighted match. Ooh, aah. Oompah! As the flames die down and the children stop crying, ladle cherries over ice cream or cake and serve. Serves 6. —*Connie Thompson*

Quick Peanut Butter Cookies

1 1/2 cups peanut butter
2 egg whites
1 cup white sugar

Mix the three ingredients thoroughly. Drop walnut-size dollops onto a greased cookie sheet and press gently with a fork. Bake 8–10 minutes at 350 degrees. Voila! Everyone loves you! (Mix the egg yolks into the dog's evening meal, or stir into milk for the cat. Might as well have the animals love you, as well.) Makes 12–16 cookies.

Shortbread

Nothing but the essential ingredients in this classic recipe. No need to run out to the grocery store.

1 1/4 cups all-purpose flour
3 tablespoons sugar
1/2 cup butter

In bowl, mix together flour and sugar. Cut in cold butter with fork or pastry knife until a crumb mixture forms. Form into a ball and knead until smooth. On an ungreased cookie sheet, roll out the ball into an 8-inch flat circle. Cut into squares or pie-shaped wedges, but do not separate. Bake at 325 degrees for 25–30 minutes. Recut cookies. Cool on cookie sheet 5 minutes, separate, then cool on wood board or wire rack. Makes 12 cookies.

Sugar Cookies

Quick and easy—and everybody loves 'em. A good recipe that the kids can help make on that rainy day at the cottage.

    1 cup butter
    1 cup sugar
    2 eggs
    1 tablespoon milk
    ½ teaspoon salt
    2 teaspoons baking powder
    1 teaspoon vanilla
    1½ cups all-purpose flour

Cream the butter and add sugar. Add beaten eggs, milk, and 1 cup of flour sifted with baking powder and salt. Add vanilla and just enough flour to form a dough that will roll easily. Chill well. Work with just a small amount of dough at a time, keeping the rest in the refrigerator. Roll out to ¼ inch, cut in any shape, and bake 10 minutes in a moderate (350 degrees) oven. Makes 16–20 cookies.

Oatmeal-Cranberry Cookies

And now for something really healthful.

    1¾ pound butter
    2½ cups packed brown sugar
    2½ cups white granulated sugar
    5 eggs
    16 cups rolled oats
    5 cups all-purpose flour
    1 tablespoon baking soda
    1 tablespoon vanilla
    1½ tablespoons salt
    4 cups dried cranberries

Step One: Preheat oven to 375 degrees. In a large bowl, cream the butter and sugars. Add 1 egg at a time, mixing after each addition, until they are well blended. Add in the oats and flour. Step Two: In a small bowl, thoroughly mix together the baking soda, 2 cups of water, vanilla, and salt. Add to the oat mixture, mix well, and add the cranberries. With teaspoon, scoop batter and drop onto a cookie sheet. Bake 10 minutes at 375 degrees. Makes 6 dozen cookies, which should last at least a day.

Chocolate Brownies

Who doesn't like chocolate brownies? Nobody, that's who. This is a great recipe to make with the kids on a rainy day.

2 cups semi-sweet chocolate chips
1 stick butter, cut into ½-inch slices
3 large eggs, beaten
1¼ cups all-purpose flour
1 cup granulated sugar
¼ teaspoon baking soda
1 teaspoon vanilla extract
½ cup chopped nuts (optional)

Preheat oven to 350 degrees. Grease a 9x13-inch baking pan. Melt 1 cup of the chocolate chips in a heavy-duty saucepan over very low heat, and stir until smooth. Then remove from heat and stir in the eggs. Next, stir in the flour, sugar, baking soda, and vanilla extract. Stir in the other cup of chocolate chips and the nuts (if desired), stirring until all the chocolate is melted. Spread the mixture evenly into the baking pan and bake for 20–22 minutes. Cool, cut, and enjoy.

Dutch Apple Tart

9-inch prepared unbaked piecrust
5 apples
1 tablespoon flour
1 cup sugar
¼ teaspoon nutmeg
2 teaspoons butter

Line pie dish with the prepared crust. Sprinkle the flour and ¼ cup of the sugar on bottom of the crust. Peel and quarter the apples and place them cut-side down. Cover with the balance of the sugar, dot with the butter, and sprinkle with the nutmeg. Bake in a moderate oven (350 degrees) about 35 minutes or until apples are baked and a rich syrup has formed. Serves 8.

Wisconsin Fudge

OK, it's doubtful that there's not a fudge shop within a three-minute drive of your cottage—but just in case . . .

    1 pound chocolate chips (dark or milk)
    1 cup butter
    8-ounce jar of marshmallow cream
    2 teaspoons vanilla
    4½ cups sugar
    1 medium-size can evaporated milk
    Chopped nuts (optional)

You'll need a mixing bowl, a cooking pot, and a baking pan for this recipe. (Sorry about that.) In a large bowl, mix together the first four ingredients. In a separate large cooking pot mix together the sugar and milk, and bring to a boil while stirring constantly. At the boil point, lower the heat and continue to cook for another 10 minutes, without stirring. Pour the milk mixture over the dry ingredients and mix well until all ingredients are well blended. If desired, add chopped nuts. Pour into a greased baking pan and refrigerate for 24 hours. Cut into pieces and wrap in cling wrap or waxed paper. Fight over who gets the biggest piece.

Strawberry Parfait

Easy? They'll never know how easy—and we'll never tell.

Crush fresh berries and mix with store-bought whipped topping and just a little honey. Perch a whole berry on top of every dish. (Serve in wine glasses and they'll be doubly impressed.)

Lime Jell-O Marshmallow Cottage Cheese Surprise!

What could be more appropriate at the cottage than a cottage cheese surprise? And what better way to end this little cookbook? We were inspired by the brilliant song of the same name ("Lime Jell-O Marshmallow Cottage Cheese Surprise") by William Bolcom, to offer our own version of this perfectly outstanding and tasteful dish.

1 small package lime Jell-O
1 cup boiling water
1 cup mini marshmallows
½ cup chocolate chips
1 cup apples, diced
½ cup celery, diced
1 cup crushed pineapple, drained
1 cup mayonnaise
1 cup cottage cheese
1 container Strawberry Cool Whip

Mix Jell-O with boiling water until dissolved. Add marshmallows and stir until they, too, dissolve. Set aside and allow to set just partially. Add all other ingredients except Cool Whip. Fold in Cool Whip gently, pour into mold, and refrigerate overnight. Voila! Could serve 6 to 64, depending on how many people refuse to eat any at all.

Index

A

B

C

MORE GREAT TITLES
FROM TRAILS BOOKS
& PRAIRIE OAK PRESS

ACTIVITY GUIDES

Biking Wisconsin: 50 Great Road and Trail Rides, *Steve Johnson*

Great Cross-Country Ski Trails: Wisconsin, Minnesota, Michigan & Ontario,
Wm. Chad McGrath

Great Iowa Walks: 50 Strolls, Rambles, Hikes, and Treks, *Lynn L. Walters*

Great Minnesota Walks: 49 Strolls, Rambles, Hikes, and Treks, *Wm. Chad McGrath*

Great Wisconsin Walks: 45 Strolls, Rambles, Hikes, and Treks, *Wm. Chad McGrath*

Horsing Around in Wisconsin, *Anne M. Connor*

Iowa Underground, *Greg A. Brick*

Minnesota Underground & the Best of the Black Hills, *Doris Green*

Paddling Illinois: 64 Great Trips by Canoe and Kayak, *Mike Svob*

Paddling Iowa: 96 Great Trips by Canoe and Kayak, *Nate Hoogeveen*

Paddling Northern Minnesota: 86 Great Trips by Canoe and Kayak,
Lynne Smith Diebel

Paddling Northern Wisconsin: 82 Great Trips by Canoe and Kayak, *Mike Svob*

Paddling Southern Wisconsin: 82 Great Trips by Canoe and Kayak, *Mike Svob*

Walking Tours of Wisconsin's Historic Towns, *Lucy Rhodes,
Elizabeth McBride, Anita Matcha*

Wisconsin's Outdoor Treasures: A Guide to 150 Natural Destinations, *Tim Bewer*

Wisconsin Underground, *Doris Green*

TRAVEL GUIDES

Classic Wisconsin Weekends, *Michael Bie*

Great Little Museums of the Midwest, *Christine des Garennes*

Great Midwest Country Escapes, *Nina Gadomski*

Great Minnesota Taverns, *David K. Wright & Monica G. Wright*

Great Minnesota Weekend Adventures, *Beth Gauper*

Great Weekend Adventures, *the Editors of Wisconsin Trails*

Great Wisconsin Romantic Weekends, *Christine des Garennes*

Great Wisconsin Taverns: 101 Distinctive Badger Bars, *Dennis Boyer*

Iowa's Hometown Flavors, *Donna Tabbert Long*

Sacred Sites of Minnesota, *John-Brian Paprock & Teresa Peneguy Paprock*

Sacred Sites of Wisconsin, *John-Brian Paprock & Teresa Peneguy Paprock*

Tastes of Minnesota: A Food Lover's Tour, *Donna Tabbert Long*

The Great Iowa Touring Book: 27 Spectacular Auto Trips, *Mike Whye*

The Great Minnesota Touring Book: 30 Spectacular Auto Trips, *Thomas Huhti*

The Great Wisconsin Touring Book: 30 Spectacular Auto Tours, *Gary Knowles*

Wisconsin Family Weekends: 20 Fun Trips for You and the Kids,
Susan Lampert Smith
Wisconsin Golf Getaways, *Jeff Mayers and Jerry Poling*
Wisconsin Lighthouses: A Photographic and Historical Guide,
Ken and Barb Wardius
Wisconsin's Hometown Flavors, *Terese Allen*
Wisconsin Waterfalls, *Patrick Lisi*
Up North Wisconsin: A Region for All Seasons, *Sharyn Alden*

HOME & GARDEN

Bountiful Wisconsin: 110 Favorite Recipes, *Terese Allen*
Codfather 2, *Jeff Hagen*
Creating a Perennial Garden in the Midwest, *Joan Severa*
Eating Well in Wisconsin, *Jerry Minnich*
Foods That Made Wisconsin Famous: 150 Great Recipes, *Richard J. Baumann*
Midwest Cottage Gardening, *Frances Manos*
North Woods Cottage Cookbook, *Jerry Minnich*
Wisconsin Country Gourmet, *Marge Snyder & Suzanne Breckenridge*
Wisconsin Garden Guide, *Jerry Minnich*

HISTORICAL BOOKS

Barns of Wisconsin, *Jerry Apps*
Duck Hunting on the Fox: Hunting and Decoy-Carving Traditions,
Stephen M. Miller
Grand Army of the Republic: Department of Wisconsin, *Thomas J. McCrory*
Portrait of the Past: A Photographic Journey Through Wisconsin 1865-1920,
Howard Mead, Jill Dean, and Susan Smith
Prairie Whistles: Tales of Midwest Railroading, *Dennis Boyer*
Shipwrecks of Lake Michigan, *Benjamin J. Shelak*
Wisconsin At War: 20th Century Conflicts Through the Eyes of Veterans, *Dr.
James F. McIntosh, M.D.*
Wisconsin's Historic Houses & Living History Museums, *Krista Finstad Hanson*
Wisconsin: The Story of the Badger State, *Norman K. Risjord*

GIFT BOOKS

Celebrating Door County's Wild Places, *The Ridges Sanctuary*
Fairlawn: Restoring the Splendor, *Tom Davis*
Madison, *Photography by Brent Nicastro*
Milwaukee, *Photography by Todd Dacquisto*
Milwaukee Architecture: A Guide to Notable Buildings, *Joseph Korom*
Spirit of the North: A Photographic Journey Through Northern Wisconsin,
Richard Hamilton Smith

The Spirit of Door County: A Photographic Essay, *Darryl R. Beers*
Uncommon Sense: The Life Of Marshall Erdman, *Doug Moe & Alice D'Alessio*

LEGENDS & LORE

Driftless Spirits: Ghosts of Southwest Wisconsin, *Dennis Boyer*
Haunted Wisconsin, *Michael Norman and Beth Scott*
The Beast of Bray Road: Tailing Wisconsin's Werewolf, *Linda S. Godfrey*
The Eagle's Voice: Tales Told by Indian Effigy Mounds, *Gary J. Maier, M.D.*
The Poison Widow: A True Story of Sin, Strychnine, & Murder, *Linda S. Godfrey*
The W-Files: True Reports of Wisconsin's Unexplained Phenomena, *Jay Rath*

YOUNG READERS

ABCs Naturally, *Lynne Smith Diebel & Jann Faust Kalscheur*
ABCs of Wisconsin, *Dori Hillestad Butler, Illustrated by Alison Relyea*
H is for Hawkeye, *Jay Wagner, Illustrated by Eileen Potts Dawson*
H is for Hoosier, *Dori Hillestad Butler, Illustrated by Eileen Potts Dawson*
Wisconsin Portraits, *Martin Hintz*
Wisconsin Sports Heroes, *Martin Hintz*
W is for Wisconsin, *Dori Hillestad Butler, Illustrated by Eileen Potts Dawson*

SPORTS

Baseball in Beertown: America's Pastime in Milwaukee, *Todd Mishler*
Before They Were the Packers: Green Bay's Town Team Days,
Denis J. Gullickson & Carl Hanson
Cold Wars: 40+ Years of Packer-Viking Rivalry, *Todd Mishler*
Downfield: Untold Stories of the Green Bay Packers, *Jerry Poling*
Great Moments in Wisconsin Sports, *Todd Mishler*
Green Bay Packers Titletown Trivia Teasers, *Don Davenport*
Mean on Sunday: The Autobiography of Ray Nitschke, *Robert W. Wells*
Mudbaths and Bloodbaths: The Inside Story of the Bears-Packers Rivalry, *Gary
D'Amato & Cliff Christl*
Packers By the Numbers: Jersey Numbers and the Players Who Wore Them, *John
Maxymuk*

OTHER

Driftless Stories, *John Motoviloff*
River Stories: Growing Up on the Wisconsin, *Delores Chamberlain*
The Wisconsin Father's Guide to Divorce, *James Novak*
Travels With Sophie: The Journal of Louise E. Wegner,
Edited by Gene L. LaBerge & Michelle L. Maurer
Trout Friends, *Bill Stokes*
Wild Wisconsin Notebook, *James Buchholz*